LIONEL EDWARDS
Master of the Sporting Scene

LIONEL EDWARDS

MASTER OF THE SPORTING SCENE

J.N.P WATSON

FOREWORD BY
THE MARQUESS OF DUFFERIN AND AVA

· THE ·
SPORTSMAN'S
PRESS
LONDON

Published by The Sportsman's Press in
1986

© J. N. P. Watson 1986

British Library Cataloguing in Publication Data

Watson, J.N.P.
Lionel Edwards: master of the sporting
scene.
1. Edwards, Lionel   2. Painters—England
—Biography
I. Title
759.2   ND497.E/

ISBN 0-948253-08-8

Printed and bound in Great Britain by
BAS Printers Limited, Over Wallop, Stockbridge Hampshire

CONTENTS

For
Country Life
with gratitude

FOREWORD

BY THE MARQUESS OF DUFFERIN AND AVA
Chairman of the British Sporting Art Trust

It is rare indeed to find such a sympathetic and illuminating treatment of any painter as this excellent biography of Lionel Edwards. John Watson has been meticulous in his research and all devotees of sporting art will be for ever in his debt.

It is all too surprising how many artists of calibre have still to be researched and written about, but no one who wishes to know about the life and work of Lionel Edwards will have to do anything other than to read this book. John Watson has managed to convey with wit and clarity the fascinating and varied life of his subject. Lionel Edwards's passion for venery, the dramatic impact of his involvement in World War I, and his constant search for perfection in his art throughout his long life are all brought vividly alive. It was said of him that 'his hunting landscapes held the heart of England', and who can disagree?

As Chairman of the British Sporting Art Trust I warmly recommend this handsomely illustrated biography as much to the new generations of sportsmen and women as to those fortunate enough to have known the magic of Lionel Edwards at first hand.

May, 1986

PREFACE

A new generation has grown up in the period that has elapsed since Lionel Edwards died. He was, in his prime, a Victorian and an Edwardian; his early art reflected the values, ideals and humour of those times. Most of his later work was seen through the eyes of a man who cherished the old modes and courtesies, disciplines and traditions, and who saw the hunting-field and the racecourse of (more or less) half-a-century ago as being at once the most beautiful and the bravest sporting arenas in the world. Those of the older generations who love his style and the aspects and scenes of his paintings will surely harbour some regret for the passing of those eras; while those who are too young to have known them will perhaps view his pictures with a nostalgia for a British landscape that was more attractive, and a country fraternity that was more warmly cohesive, than the ones with which they are now familiar. As for LE, he would give a wan headshake if he returned for glimpses of the relatively inelegant and mannerless world in which we now live. At the same time he would applaud with his ready smile the Englishman's prevailing high enthusiasm for horse and hound and his continued spirit of the old foxhunter's cry — 'Be with them we *will!*'

I have admired Lionel Edwards's work for as long as I can remember. The walls of my room at school, like those of many of my friends, were adorned with his prints. It made a refreshing and exciting break to raise the eyes from the evening study of, say, dry Latin or Greek verse to one of those pictures and gallop in the mind's eye across the Belvoir Vale, or look down with him from Rankboro gorse or career over the Galway Blazers' walls or face the Whissendine. In those days I would never have dreamed I would have the privilege of putting a book such as this together. I am happy to admit that it is composed more of the wisdom, wit and memory of his own pen and lips, and of those who knew him well, than with my own comment; and my thanks are particularly due to his daughter, Miss Marjorie Edwards, who read my typescripts and who gave me several pieces of family information (a most generous favour considering she was still busy at the time with her own memoir of her father). I am also grateful to Miss Edwards and Messrs Lindsay and Ken Edwards for allowing me to quote from their father's books and to use illustrations from them. My thanks are due, too, to the owners of the many paintings shown here for their permission to reproduce them. To all those friends and acquaintances of Lionel Edwards, who entertained me in their homes to talk about him, particularly Mrs Denis Aldridge, Lieutenant-Colonel C. G. M. Gordon, Mrs H. G. Gregson, the Hon. Lady Stucley and the Hon. Aylmer Tryon. To Mr Charles Chafer for the memoir which he sent me, to Mrs Critchley-Salmonson for her note on Peter Biegel, and to Mr Roy Heron for his notes. To the following for their help in the provision of illustrations: the Editor of *Country Life*, the British Sporting Art Trust (especially Dr Robert Fountain), Messrs Spink and Son, the Richard Green Gallery (especially Mr William Byfield), the William Marler Gallery, the Tryon and Moorland Galleries (especially Mr Claude Berry and the Hon. David Bigham), Guy Morrison, His Grace the Duke of Northumberland, the Hon. Lady Stucley, Mr Ralph Gilbey, Mrs H. G. Gregson, Mrs P. M. Tarlton, Mrs J. Tice, Captain Gordon Fergusson, Major John Berkeley, Mr Luke Sykes, Mr Jim Meads, Mrs Denis Aldridge, Mrs Peter Biegel and Colonel James Hamilton-Russell (commanding the Household Cavalry, 1983–86). And, most warmly of all, my wife, Lavinia, who typed both the manuscript and all the copious correspondence connected with the book.

J.N.P.W.
Pannett's Shipley
Horsham
Sussex

Lionel Edwards at work

I

YOUTH

Hunting is the noblest exercise
Makes men laborious, active, wise,
Brings health and doth the spirits delight,
It helps the hearing and the sight;
It teaches arts that never slip
The memory — good horsemanship
Search, sharpness, courage and defence
All chaseth all ill-habits thence.

Ben Johnson

Carriage and Pair, 1900

'A great number of people of all ages and of all countries appreciate Lionel Edwards as an artist — to myself, as to many others, the greatest sporting artist of all time — but those who had the good fortune to know him well knew him not only as an artist but as a very great gentleman. His most outstanding merit was his modesty, or perhaps his natural kindness. For I never heard him speak one word of malice of anyone. . . . He was a great man, at home in any company; a man full of understanding, a most amusing story teller and a grand companion.'

'Dalesman' (C. N. de Courcy Parry) Master of Foxhounds and sporting writer.

'It is the special triumph of Mr Lionel Edwards that, in all his painting and drawing, not only does he show us the truth but mankind itself instantly knows it to be true. . . . His hunting landscapes hold the heart of England.'

'Crascredo' (Equestrian writer of the 1920s and '30s)

'Lionel knew more about the hunting countries of the British Isles than any other living man, having hunted in them and painted them all his life. . . . In his paintings of Exmoor he not only captured the very essence of the moor but also, through long and patient hours of observation of their forms and habits, probably portrayed the red deer better than any other artist before or since.'

Mrs Denis Aldridge (LE named her and her husband as his best friends)

'Whereas he loved painting he loved hunting even more, and while he enjoyed the ride, he essentially rode to hunt . . . houndwork fascinated him.'

Charles Chafer (Master of Foxhounds and patron)

'If asked who knew most about the hunting countries of the British Isles, I would say, without hesitation, Lionel Edwards. He has been a hunting man all his life. . . . We are indeed fortunate that a man with such a wonderful eye for country has been able to capture for us the atmosphere of each. . . .'

Hon. Aylmer Tryon (Founder of the Tryon Gallery)

'At once a great sporting artist and a most likeable character.'

Jack Gilbey (Patron)

[13]

'He immortalised the foxhunting scenes and personalities of this century as no other artist has done before or since.'

Daphne Moore (Sporting writer and authority on hounds)

'A most charming man, shy and unassuming, but always very kindly and cheerful. . . . I have always thought his genius has been greatly underestimated.'

Hon. Lady Stucley (Patron)

'Lionel Edwards was not only Britain's outstanding sporting artist but, in my opinion, he was also one of the finest landscape painters this country has ever produced.'

Joan Wanklyn (Equestrian and military artist)

'First and foremost a foxhunting man, he drew and painted what he loved doing and his remarkable eye for country was that of the man who sees the landscape from the saddle. . . . His outstanding ability was for the re-creation of the exciting atmosphere of the hunt, as it is felt both by those who take part in it and by the country folk for whom it is a familiar experience.'

Obituary in *The Times*, April 14, 1966

Those are a mere fraction of the tributes showered on Lionel Edwards by people close to him and close to the realm of field sports. The claim made so often on his behalf — that he was the greatest hunting artist of all time — must, by virtue of popular referendum, surely go unchallenged? None of the 19th-century giants, Alken, Marshall, Cooper, Davis or Ferneley, can rival him, for none of them captured at once the melodrama, the winter ambience, the glory and the consummate truth of the British and Irish hunting scene in all its moods as Edwards did. He himself was of the opinion that George Stubbs's best painting was *The Grosvenor Hunt*. But that artist's relatively few hunting pictures were — like those of Munnings — really rather too formal, a little unreal, compared with his other equestrian and rural subjects. So not even the great Stubbs competes. And if any of Edwards's celebrated contemporaries, Aldin, Armour, Haigh, Holiday or 'Snaffles' (Charles Johnson Payne) were asked to name the world's supreme hunting artist there is little doubt they would, with one voice, cry 'LE!'

It was not simply that he was a superb painter *per se*, coupled with the facts that he was, at one time, a professional horsemaster and his favourite occupation was riding to hounds. He possessed many more strings to his bow, many other assets.

He was passionately fond of all animals and contrived to feel, while he painted, with their senses, and he relished the aura, the smell, sound and animation of stable and kennel.

Moreover, he knew as much, if not more, about hounds and venery and the wiles and ways of fox, deer and hare than most Masters of hounds of his day – and than many of their huntsmen, too. It was his delight to mix with, talk freely with, all manner of country folk. The rise and fall, the strength and beauty of hill and valley seemed to flow through his limbs, as though, like electric currents, they became a part of him – and returned, vibrant and glowing, though his pencil and the hairs of his brush to the canvas. He lent the knowledge of a serious farmer to his work, while his remarkable sense of history enabled him to envisage, in one majestic sweep, the unfolding of the heritage of British field sports, horse transport and agricultural life. He possessed in full measure what the Spanish philosopher, Ortega y Gasset, called 'the habits of alertness and acuity that link the hunter in participation with all creation'.

The source of a man's gifts, the derivation of his talent, the fount of his natural inheritance is an absorbing study in itself. What proportion, in this instance or that, springs from the genes, how much from early environment? In the case of Lionel Edwards we must look first at the interests and motivations of his father, Dr James Edwards, who, being five years old when the Battle of Waterloo was fought, was 68 when Lionel, the youngest of all his children, was born.

According to LE, his father, a citizen of Chester and a physician with a particular expertise in stomach troubles, could scarcely wait to save sufficient money from his practice to retire to a life of farming, hunting, fishing and gardening. Indeed James Edwards – the restlessly energetic man that Lionel was also to be – while still a practitioner, ran a small farm at Rowton; kept horses at the Swan Inn, Tarporley (of hunt club fame); was out with hounds whenever they met and he was free; and, in the summer months, devoted much of his time to his garden and the trout-filled rivers.

It was following the death of his first wife, Jane (née Maine) and her son Gamul, that Dr Edwards gave up his Chester practice, bought Benarth Hall ('in semi-ruinous condition') and its estate, near Conway, in north Wales, and moved in there with his daughter, Mary, who, notwithstanding their age gaps, was to become very close

Dr James Edwards. 'There is no doubt at all,' wrote LE, 'where my love of hunting comes from.'

to Lionel. Dr Edwards then married Eliza Ellen Smith ('of whom I know nothing', says Lionel, 'except that she died in childbirth and I have her silver'). Dr Edwards remained an irrepressible sportsman. From Wales he travelled to Leamington each winter to hunt with the dashing Warwickshire. It was while hacking back to stables one windy evening from a day with that pack that he made the decision to abandon foxhunting; and with good reason. He overheard one young thruster say to another as they, too, turned their horses' heads for home: 'The old doctor's getting a wonderful eye for a gap!' To earn a reputation for avoiding obstacles was more than James Edwards could bear. But, somehow or other his sport must continue. So he put together a pack of beagles* and, riding a quiet pony, hunted the country above Conway Bay with a new gusto.

*LE tells us those hounds were eventually sold to Sir Vincent Corbet, of Acton Reynolds, and were probably passed on to the Mostyn family.

The Ledbury at Staunton
(Watercolour)

Racing in the Wet, 1907
(Watercolour)

Cubhunting with the North Cotswold (Charcoal and watercolour heightened with bodycolour on buff paper)

The Quorn towards Ashby de la Zouche, 1917 (Watercolour)

During the 1850s Dr Edwards took a third wife, Lionel's mother, Harriet Maine, a cousin of the first Mrs Edwards. Although sharing her husband's interests and great spirit and energy, if not his unqualified devotion to north Wales, she appears to have been a more sophisticated person than him, a woman who demanded a frequent change of scene and cherished London as well as the rural life. Harriet was in her twenties, James in his late forties when they married, yet it seems to have proved a harmonious union. The eldest child of their partnership, Fitz, was 19 and already in the Army by the time Lionel, the last of their five sons, came into the world, in 1878. He was only seven when his father died.

Lionel was born at Clifton, adjacent to Bristol, but had no recollections of that vicinity. His early background and memories are of the Welsh hills and the men and hounds who hunted them, the wild skies above them, the hill farms with their plough horses and cattle breeds, sheep flocks and collie dogs, Welsh voices singing, dazzling moorland colours and his old father's farming and sporting activities. 'My nursery looked across a mile of river estuary which became mudflats and sandbanks at low water' he remembered half a century later. 'It was haunted by duck and sea-fowl, whose plaintive cries became woven into my childish dreams. Even today the cry of the oyster-catcher, the curlew, or the little dotterels and sandpipers, make the years fall away, and for fleeting seconds I am a child again.' The sounds of horn-music and hound-song, the whinney and echo of hooves on cobbles were fondly recalled in those boyish ears, too. 'There is no doubt at all where my love of hunting comes from,' he wrote. 'But it is probably further fortified by the fact that it was the custom of those days to put children out to a wet-nurse. I understand that mine was both the daughter and the wife of a coachman so probably I imbibed the love of horses with my foster-mother's milk.'

The family was now short of money and 'consequently my education was of a halting and irregular character'. Self-education was helping to fill the gap. He had formed the habit of sketching animals and people by the age of five. His very first hunting picture, drawn at that age, was of a huntsman accompanied by a single hound. (He gave the sketch, much later, to Jack Gilbey.) He was a strong, active, upright lad who claimed to 'possess certain leanings towards soldiering'. The only evidence he offers for this is that 'I remember going to a volunteer assault-at-arms.'

Clearly the fascination with militaria and soldiering, which stayed with him from

[17]

boyhood to the grave, stemmed much more from his love of tradition, national ritual and custom and the kinship, of field sports and war, than it did from a genuine interest in the practical aspects of the Army. His father implanted in his mind a great sense of the romance of England's past. The Edwardses were very proud of the fact that the blood of a Chester family, called Gamul, flowed in their veins. James Edwards's son by his first marriage was christened Robert William Gamul.

Their ancestor, Sir Francis Gamul, is on record as entertaining, at his Chester house, Charles I, and was at the King's side during the Royal defeat at Rowton Heath, the result of the King's attempt to relieve Chester in September, 1645. Sir Francis's son, Thomas, was killed in the battle, aged 18. Charles gave Gamul an ebony stick, the symbol of a privileged attendant, which passed down the Edwards family to Lionel, together with a portrait of the Royalist Knight; but 'it has mysteriously disappeared', LE regretted, 'presumably stolen'.

Anyhow, Mrs Edwards declined the place offered by Albert Wood to her budding young limner, when he was nine years old, in a Paris art school, and eventually sent him to an army crammer. Perhaps she was persuaded by her soldier son, Fitz. However, Tom Sheddan, to whose London academy Lionel was dispatched, decided that he 'either had no brains or, alternatively, refused to exert them; and reported very tactfully that I seemed to be more interested in artistic than military matters'. It was

[18]

not considered respectable in those days for the sons of gentlefolk to become artists, but, as Lionel says, 'my mother was sufficiently strong-minded to overcome Victorian prejudices and let me study at an art school'. He believed that 'any such artistic talent as I possess comes from my grandmother, Ann Robertson, of Edinburgh (died 1857), a friend and pupil of George Romney'. He was told 'she had considerable talent as well as personal beauty'. It was not for nothing that he had been christened Lionel Dalhousie Robertson.

He joined Frank Calderon's school of animal painting in Baker Street and was to admit a large debt of thanks to both Calderon and his anatomical lecturer, Dr Armstead. Calderon also ran a school studio in Midhurst, Sussex, where Cecil Aldin, Lionel's senior by eight years, had attended his classes. Calderon, the son of an R.A. and grandson, on his mother's side, of another R.A., had a promising early career as an artist. (His first painting to be exhibited at the Royal Academy, when he was 16 years old, was bought by Queen Victoria.) He enjoyed a brilliant reputation as a teacher, too. But Lionel did not think the scholarships won from there stood him in particularly good stead since. ' . . . Being in straitened circumstances . . . they encouraged me to walk before I could crawl, and I endeavoured to earn my living by drawing long before I had learnt to draw, with the result that I turned out some dreadful trash'.

On reflection, however, he was inclined to think that 'the quick press work, that the earning of money entailed, did me a certain amount of good, as it requires both speed and quick decision to sketch contemporary events in competition with the press photographer. . . . That period was an invaluable experience to a budding artist with leanings towards journalism.' Most evenings found him figure-drawing at Heatherleys.

Young Edwards spent the years 1897 to 1903 in London with a studio – sublet to him by a cousin, Miss Halkett, herself an artist – in Holland Street, off Camden Hill Road, Kensington, 'in a back room overlooking a mews'. One of his early heroes, Randolph Caldecott, was the previous tenant. Although Lionel was physically strong, as well as emotionally and morally tough, his health was none too good in youth, and his doctor – swearing by the old adage 'live in the saddle! whoever heard of a bilious post boy?' – prescribed 'horse exercise'. He had ridden in childhood in quiet Wales; nothing would stop him riding in youth in turbulent London.

The man who hired him his first mount came late one night demanding more money, and Lionel finished the brisk exchange by purchasing the horse for £15,

[19]

a sum he could ill afford. But where to stable the animal? The premises of his aunt, Lady Maine (wife of a celebrated lawyer, Sir Henry) — with whom his mother, her step-sister, always stayed when in London — was the answer. But she did not know it. Lionel squared her coachman, 'who got ticked off' he remembers, 'for the unaccountable increase in the forage bills'.

He retained a vivid image of the premises. 'There were two doors, one which led into the cobble-stoned mews and the other to the stairs which led up to the coachman's quarters, for he and his family lived above his charges. I expect modern sanitary inspectors would condemn this system' (he was writing in the 1950s); 'but it certainly was not noticeable that the usually large families of coachmen were any less healthy than those of other and better-housed families. Stuffy his quarters were, and more especially so his stables, where a naked gas jet flared all day long. The heat largely accounted for the lovely satin-like coats of the carriage horses, and — combined with unnecessarily tight bearing reins — was why they so frequently went wrong in the wind.'

He recalls the huge hay wagons rolling into London, 'drawn by two or three horses, plodding slowly up to Covent Garden, their drivers often fast asleep'. In the summer freshly-cut grass and lucerne would arrive for London's huge horse population, Lionel noting that 'economical people kept this too long so that it was heated, which was responsible for many equine deaths from colic. . . . In the morning the first sound I heard was the clatter of horses' hooves and the swish of water as carriages were washed down, while in summer time a strong smell of horse urine ascended and entered my bedroom windows. Not that I ever objected to it. . . . I remember that in the dog-days of the season the London streets all smelt of hot tar and horse. A country squire of my acquaintance was quite unable to face London in the season (much to the annoyance of his wife) as the latter smell gave him horse asthma.'

He was to remember 'with distinct nostalgia, many sights and sounds that have departed from London, even such trivial things as the almost uncanny silence when iron-tyred vehicles were driven over the fifty yards of straw laid down in the road in front of a house where a sick man lay. . . .' And the hansom cab days, when 'providing you picked up a cabby with a well-bred horse in the shafts you could get from Kensington to Paddington or St Pancras a great deal quicker than you can now in a taxi, the reason being that the traffic was less dense'. He was to miss 'the Dalmatian dog running not beside but under my lady's victoria; the bright ribbons and rosettes in her horses' brow-bands; and the tiny "Tiger" standing in front of the phaeton

LE, 19-year-old art student, with his first horse, bought for £15

pair, or sitting with folded arms when she drove herself'.

A morning in Kensington Square remained vividly imprinted on his mind's eye. 'Every house had a window-box, gay with flowers. Most houses had bright-coloured sun blinds, and a smart carriage and pair waited outside more than one door – sleek bay horses, shining harness and smart servants in new liveries. At the end of the square stood two hansom cabs with good-looking old screws in the shafts. . . . Outside another house two hacks were being led up and down; judging by the groom's stable dress they were hirelings, for only a few people brought their own hacks, as well as their carriage horses, up to London for the season. In addition a butcher's cart, with a smart cob in the shafts, rattled by, delivering a late order. The London butchers were famous for their smart cobs and turnouts. The drivers in their blue aprons and smooth plastered-down hair, sitting high above their box-like vehicles were great artists in driving at top speed through thick traffic. . . .'

A bicycle was Lionel's conveyance for commuting to Calderon's; but he rode in Rotten Row three mornings a week and out to the country at weekends. He made use of his nag for quite short journeys, too. He was reminded, much later in life,

[21]

by the proprietor of Reeves's art shop in High Street, Kensington, that he arrived on horseback to make his purchases there.

In those 1890s it was, as Lionel points out, 'quite usual to hunt from London by train, and pink-coated horsemen and their rugged-up horses could be seen almost any morning during the winter months at Euston or Paddington station'. He never came across anyone trying to hack west or north to meets, but the southern hunt countries were more accessible. The London horseman, crossing the Thames via Hammersmith Bridge was 'soon riding through countrified Richmond and Mortlake'. Lionel, who was growing more enthusiastic by the week on his equitation, bought another horse 'out of a hansom cab on Westminster bridge' for around the same price as the first.

Hacking from Kensington early one morning he rode to meet the Surrey staghounds at Esher, only to find the meet cancelled owing to the death of one of the hunt's leading members. Lionel's friend and fellow animal-artist, Cecil Aldin, was more fortunate. 'It was from Bedford Park, Chiswick, that I began my life as a sportsman', he tells us in *Time I Was Dead*. 'For this great day I started by road to the meet, exactly like the renowned Mr Jorrocks of St Botolph's Lane, to hunt with a Surrey pack. . . .' Aldin, unlike Lionel, got his day's hunting. 'I imagine the late Cecil Aldin was the last person to hack to a meet from Bedford Park', hazards Lionel;

'but in point of distance I beat him and I should think no one has since tried to emulate us.'

There was an accident on one of the occasions that Lionel rode to visit Aldin, at his Bedford Park house. Lionel tied his horse by the reins to Aldin's studio door. Aldin's bulldog, in a nervous moment, jumped from a chair, bringing down an arrangement of artists' props, which was 'too much for my gee on the other side of the glass, and he jumped back, pulling the door off its hinges and dragging it across the yard'.

Polo — having been introduced into the western world via British cavalry officers stationed at Aldershot in 1869 — was a relatively new game. But, from the 1870s its popularity spread like wildfire among rich young sportsmen, who were applying by the dozen for membership of the fashionable London clubs, Hurlingham, Roehampton and Ranelagh; and south London stables were crowded with their ponies. Lionel never played — he could not afford it — but brother Fitz, an officer in the Poona Light Horse, sent him graphic accounts of the game from India, while the youthful artist was fascinated by the equine rhythm and bustle of the chukkas.

He cycled to one or other of those three clubs regularly, and could be seen standing in the pony lines or on the sides of the grounds with sketchbook and pencil, drawing, observing and re-drawing by the hour. When Captain E. D. Miller's classic *Modern Polo* was published Lionel was among the first to buy a copy. Its cover soon bore the bold imprint of a horse's hoof, because, a few days later, he skidded his bicycle under a horse bus with the book in his pocket.

Cecil Aldin drew a vivid pen-picture of the bicycle craze of the 1890s. The roads of some London districts, he says, 'were crowded with fat and thin, short and long men, boys and girls, learning or becoming expert at the art of taking exercise on the new low bicycles. Nightly the talk in the houses and clubs was about the latest gears or ball-bearings, the newest types of handle-bars, lamps or pneumatic tyres. The bicycle rage became a fever. Everyone caught it, from children only just able to walk, to grandmothers. Between eleven and twelve o'clock in the morning the broad, smooth drives at Battersea were so congested with bicycle-wheels that special side-track sections were kept for "beginners only". One saw stout old dowagers being instructed and held up by even fatter stud-grooms and butlers, while some of the great-great-grandparents attempted wobbly performances on tricycles. A very few of the more daring of the younger set appeared in bloomers, and were considered almost outside the pale by their elders. . . .'

[23]

A Cecil Aldin cartoon
c. 1900: *The Bicycle
Craze*. (From Aldin's
Time I Was Dead)

In 1898 Lionel was elected to the London Sketch Club (whose meeting-place was the Modern Gallery, New Bond Street) and at the age of 20, was easily the youngest member. The club's leading lights were Cecil Aldin, Phil May, Dudley Hardy, John Hassall, Lance ('Thack') Thackeray, Lee Hankey and George Haite. Aldin and Hassall were founder members. The one for whom Lionel reserved most admiration was Phil May, who 'made a lot of money, which he gave away faster than he could collect, he being the most generous and erratic person. He was a brilliant draughtsman . . .' And, as Lionel also reminds us 'somewhat overfond of the bottle'.

On one occasion, described by Lionel, May, wanting a policeman as a model, secured the services of one, but being tipsy accosted several more, to whom he gave his address, and, on returning home, found a bevy of them waiting at his studio. Aldin gives similar examples of May's character. 'I happened to be walking up the Strand a year or so before he died, when I was hailed from a passing hansom cab, and as it drew up at the kerb, recognised Phil's plain face. Flinging open the doors he jumped out, wearing a pair of the noisiest check trousers I have ever seen. No one could ever overlook Phil's breeches. . . . Nothing could ever ruffle his delightful disposition, and, whether lit up or sober he was always the same, generous, kind-hearted, open-handed friend. . . . In those days no man could possibly meet another without taking him in somewhere to have a drink. It would have been considered

Self-portrait by Phil May. 'The one for whom LE reserved most admiration'

grossly rude not to do so, and Phil was a great upholder of this system. Hardly had he alighted than he dragged me by the arm telling the smiling cabman to wait, and made a bee-line for Romano's which happened to be almost touching us. . . .'

Lionel's first drawings for the press were of the wild cattle of Chillingham, in north Northumberland, work that was promptly accepted by the Editor of *Country Life*, the magazine with which he enjoyed the closest relationship throughout his life. (LE refers to the Editor as 'Mr Vincent', although the founder and proprietor of *Country Life*, Edward Hudson, was in fact still very much in command at that time.)

Having successfully applied to the owner of the cattle, Lord Tankerville, the forthright art student was at first dismissed by the keeper because he had no written permit. Back he went to Tankerville – 'in trepidation, as his aged lordship was probably by then having a siesta'. Anyhow 'the old gentleman was courtesy itself' and Lionel strode back to the heath and obtained his sketches at the cautious distance of eighty yards, lying prone in the bracken. 'I can still see,' he recorded forty years later, 'the marvellous colour of that August day as the sun sank behind the distant hills, and the wild cattle leisurely wending their way . . . to drink in the pool at the foot of the park.' (This was another early portrait which he gave to Jack Gilbey.)

While revelling in the spirit and friendships of Calderon's school and the camaraderie of the London Sketch Club, the creativity of his Holland Street studio,

[25]

First sketch in the
field: *Chillingham Bulls
Fighting*

his weekend exursions, Hyde Park 'horse exercise' and visits to the polo grounds
and racecourses, Lionel freely admitted to detesting the great metropolis. In those
six years however, holidays found him travelling with his ever restless mother ('the
old lady being one of those who liked constant change of scene'). A visit to Coxwold,
Yorkshire brought him his first day's foxhunting, when a farmer lent him a pony
for a day with the Sinnington. 'It refused to pass a donkey on a moorland path',
he notes, 'much to my annoyance'. Nevertheless he was obviously at once 'bitten
by the magic of the chase'; for, while in Yorkshire, he proceeded to take other days
with the Badsworth and the Fitzwilliam (Wentworth).

Mother and son travelled to Dulverton and then on to Barnstaple and Lynton,
where Lionel was introduced to the Exmoor with which he was to become so intimate,
and also to the excitements of staghunting. He quickly made friends with the Bawdens,
a farming family of Hollowcombe, Hawkridge, 'whose youngest son guided me on
a borrowed pony across the boundless heather, a land where nothing breaks the
surface or measures the view for the stranger, one vast stretch of open treeless
country. . . .' The youthful guide was Ernest Bawden, 'the possessor', reckoned Lionel,
'of indomitable pluck and perseverance', and who went on to serve twelve years

Brush for the Lady, 1903

The White Hart, 1902

[27]

as whipper-in to the Devon and Somerset Staghounds – under the Mastership of Robert Sanders (Lord Bayford) – and took over as huntsman in 1916.

'Staghunting is a sport you either love or hate,' he said in hindsight. 'It is quite unlike foxhunting, and therefore no comparison should, or can, be made. The late Ernest Bawden was probably the greatest huntsman that hunt has ever had, yet I personally enjoyed staghunting more before his day when the chase was run much slower, and it was conducted more on old-fashioned lines and less like a "quick thing" with foxhounds. Moreover, I think it was more fair to the deer, for whom, farmer though I be, I have a sneaking affection. . . . The early morn is the most likely time to see a stag. With the sun shining on his red-gold coat, his antlers full grown . . . he looks a grand beast as he stalks slowly across the bright green grass, leaving his tracks clearly in the dew, and the long shadows of morning behind him. He really looks what the old chronicler describes as "the most stateliest beast that doth go upon the earth, for he doth carry majesty in his countenance. . . ."'

In 1902, Fitz Edwards arrived on leave from India, bought a couple of horses from Aldridge's market and took them down to Porlock, where both brothers hunted them. When one of the hunters developed a sore on the withers, Lionel exercised him bareback. It was something of a red-letter day when he converged with the Devon and Somerset hounds running down from Dunkery into Horner. And away he went. 'Now it is quite easy', he explained, 'to sit a horse bareback at the gallop, and on the flat, but it is a devastating experience to do so downhill at any pace faster than a walk. Coming down from Webber's Post to Horner Mill I spent some ludicrous and uncomfortable minutes as I couldn't hold my horse and, in any case, dared not stop as I discovered the hunted stag was at my heels on this narrow path. . . .'

The stag concerned was held at bay by the pack 'for some minutes before the huntsman, Sidney Tucker, could dispatch him'. The scene provided Lionel with his first staghunting picture. Taking heart from the sale of it he held his first exhibition – at the parish room, Porlock, which he rented from the vicar. The success of that paid for his hunting holiday 'and even for hiring an extra horse or two'.

Death and injury, however, were rarely to be his themes. Instinct told him they were not subjects that would appeal to most British sportsmen. As a young man he made the apt observation that the blood and gore and terror of the chase belonged much more to the Continental school of animal art, whose pundits relished scenes of wounded, agonised hounds snarling around a blood-stained boar or deer, whereas the old British Masters 'all depicted the human element as their subject, or else horse

October on Exmoor. 'A land where nothing breaks the surface or measures the view for the stranger', LE described the moor. 'One vast stretch of open treeless country'

and hound – the quarry being merely an accessory. The stressing of death of the hunted animal is foreign to the ideas of English sportsmen. . . .'

He finally shook the dust of London off his feet in 1903, or thereabouts, settling in his mother's house in north Wales for a couple of years. Through the patronage and friendship of Clarence Whaite, President of the Royal Cambrian Society, he was soon elected a member, although he was still only 25.

In 1904 he went on an expedition to Oxfordshire with a landscape painter of the Glasgow school, Harry Spence, who was '. . . the first person to make me really use my eyes. Most of us think we can see, so long as we don't have to wear glasses, but it is not so, and Spence quickly disabused me of that idea. Remarkably few people are observant. . . . Still fewer seem to be able to see colour, except in its most rudimentary form. I have heard people exclaim at the beauty of a scene on the "flickers" in technicolour, yet to the artist's trained eye the lack of subtlety and gradation of tones makes the "picture" appear like the first efforts of young children with coloured chalks, and not in the least like Nature. . . . I don't know how the world at large rated Harry Spence's art, but personally I think it was a privilege to have worked in one's youth with one who painted all the time because he liked it.'

[29]

Lionel cycled many miles to be at the South Oxfordshire meets. Walter Kyte was huntsman. 'He had a lovely voice and it really was a musical treat to hear him draw a covert and find a fox.' It seems that, already, LE's first idea of heaven was to ride to hounds, to smell the odours, see the sights and hear the orchestra of the hunting field. Then to capture the scenes on his sketch pads and canvases as quickly as he could.

Sunday Morning

47

[30]

II

MARRIAGE AND WAR

Always our fathers were hunters, lords of the pitiless spear,
Chasing in English woodlands the wild white ox and the deer,
Feeling the edge of their knife-blades, trying the pull of their bows,
At a sudden foot in the forest thrilling to 'Yonder he goes!'

Safe for the space of a summer the cubs may tumble and play,
Boldly from April to August the dog-fox chooses his way;
But soon as the beech-leaf reddens, soon as the chill wind blows,
He must steal cat-foot, listening, ready for 'Yonder he goes . . .'

Not for the lust of killing, not for the places of pride,
Not for the hate of the hunted, we English saddle and ride,
But because in the gift of our fathers the blood in our veins that flows
Must answer for ever and ever the challenge of 'Yonder he goes!'
                                                    Will H. Ogilvie

Second Horsemen (From
*Sketches in Stable and
Kennel*)

Going Away
(Watercolour)

Full Cry, c. 1920
(Watercolour)

Last Fence (Point to Point)

an ounce of blood's worth a pound of bone!

Lionel Edwards

The Last Fence, c. 1920
An ounce of blood's
worth a pound of bone!
(Watercolour)

LE was 27 when he married the love of his London days, Ethel Ashness Wells. She was the daughter of the retired director of a brewing firm, but she brought little money to the marriage. Ethel's more important and significant assets were that she not only shared her husband's interests but was prepared to link her star to his life's aspirations. She was a girl of great animation and zest, she loved every aspect of life in the country and was passionately keen on hunting. She rode sidesaddle and rode beautifully and courageously. Furthermore, she possessed a most perceptive eye for the composition of drawings and paintings, and, thoughout her life, would be at once the wisest, severest and most positive critic of her husband's work.

Their first house was at Boars Hill, near Radley, Oxfordshire, where they proceeded to hunt on an income of £500 a year. 'To start with we were too broke to keep horses', said Lionel. But they were fortunate in having a sporting relation, Lady Preston, for a generous neighbour, whose husband, Sir Frederick, hunted his pack of harriers between Abingdon, Didcot and Wantage. Sir Frederick mounted the Edwardses from his stables throughout their Oxfordshire sojourn. They also followed the Old Berkshire hounds (then under the Mastership of Sir William Tyrwhitt-Drake).

They had, LE assures us, 'an astonishing lot of fun. . . . You can provided you

Sugar, 1908

[33]

'Set himself the task and the goal of earning his living primarily as an artist of the chase'.
The Quorn at Prince of Wales covert

have mutual tastes. It meant, of course, doing everything on the cheap. No groom to take over dirty and tired horses at the end of the day, but cleaning horses and tack ourselves, and no bath or tea until we had finished. It was hard work but worth it. I had no studio, but worked in an old carpenter's shop, which had no top light – only a large side window.'

Already, it seemed, the die was cast for Lionel Edwards. Since he felt himself to be more closely at one with the world in the hunting-field than anywhere else, he set himself the task and the goal of earning his living primarily as an artist of the chase. Apart from his devotion to the sport he firmly believed in the virtue of specialisation. 'With the age of man limited to three score years and ten', he advised, 'taking pains is an absolute necessity. It is impossible to master many subjects and in art, as in medicine, the specialist always comes to the top. The would-be artist should, I think, take up one or two subjects only and make them his own. The public are quick enough to spot whether one really knows the subject one is depicting.

'On the other hand there are artists who would say that specialisation is nonsense, and that, given a sufficiently high technical skill an artist ought to be able to depict what he sees in front of him. This would probably be the view of the old, long-haired, large-tie variety – the kind that a friend of mine with no artistic taste calls a "real artist". Up to a point this is correct . . . but directly an artist tackles a more intricate

[34]

subject, such as a landscape, especially one including human figures or animals, he will make errors — more quickly spotted by the public than by himself — if he has not expert knowledge, other than the handling of paint.

'For example, when looking at an excellent study of a plough team at work, a spectator remarked: "I daresay it's quite a good picture, but I should hate to have it, as I should everlastingly be annoyed by it". The artist had depicted the ploughman driving his team without any plough lines (reins). Now all this applies to what is known as representational art, which the modern critic is inclined to damn with faint praise, but as I am talking about how to make a living, perhaps Art with a large A is out of place.

'If the capacity for taking pains is needed in such cases, how infinitely more so must it be for the illustrator who, in addition to a knowledge of his subject, must have a journalist's mind, in other words the capacity to put it across to the public. . . . Supposing field sports to be an artist's special line . . . in addition to technical skill he will require knowledge of human and animal anatomy, venery, equitation, saddlery, and contemporary costume — this last is full of traps! . . . I believe it to be beyond

Gilbert Holiday. 'Almost the first artist', in Edwards's opinion, 'to master the photographic action, which we have become so accustomed to see in the daily and weekly press'

the power of any artist to depict field sports correctly unless he has taken part in them for some years himself. This is probably the reason why the ranks of sporting artists are not quite so overcrowded as every other branch of the profession.'

Soon after the turn of the century, artists such as 'Snaffles', Aldin and Armour, whose early pictures showed animals in the conventional *ventre à terre* movement, were addressing themselves to the problem of how to come to terms with what instantaneous photography was showing them and their public. For Edwards, as a serious equestrian and canine artist, this was a matter of the greatest importance. So he was particularly busy during those halcyon days before the First World War devising a style and gambits of his own to convey impressions of movement and speed, the hectic momentum and hurly-burly of the chase.

One of the strongest influences on his success in coping with the problem was his friendship, dating from that time, with Gilbert Holiday. 'To my mind' (he was to state in the 1940s), 'Holiday was almost the first artist to master the photographic action, which we have become so accustomed to seeing in the daily and weekly press. By this I mean animals in motion as seen by the camera and not the artist's

[36]

entirely conventional rendering, with which our immediate forefathers were perfectly satisfied. Now so accustomed have we become to the strange actions seen by the camera, but not by us (as its lens is very much faster than our eyes), that it is the old positions that seem absurd. Holiday, by clever manipulation of dust or mud and the consequent blurring of outlines, was able to give a tremendous sense of speed. When handling a mass of horsemen he was even better, and he would use even the most grotesque positions with success.'

Of course the 'old positions' – the rocking-horse gallops – did not seem at all 'absurd' to either the previous generations of sporting artists or their patrons or critics. Had one of the Sartorius family or the Alkens been suddenly projected into the 20th century and confronted by a photograph of galloping horses for the first time they would doubtless have expressed a very sharp interest. But they certainly would not have admitted they had been in error all along. Far from it. 'Oh yes, of course, we are perfectly aware that animals do not career across the land without flexing their legs under their bodies', they would say; 'we have no doubt that your photograph is the correct image; but that does not make it "sporting art". Your picture is graceless, it does not do justice to the fine lithe beasts; and, above all, *it does not convey a sense of speed.* Our patrons would never accept that ugly jumble of legs.'

This concept died hard – half a century after the camera began to show quite different actions from those portrayed by the sporting artists. Edwards was fascinated by the development of photography and the influence of the camera (that captured fast movement) on artistic concepts. The photographic evolution was relatively quick, but the lessons were slow to be learned in the world of art. Louis Daguerre began his experiments in 1824, being partnered, from 1826, by J. N. Niépce, whose son Isidore carried on the good work alongside his cousin, Claude Niépce de Saint-Victor, the inventor of photography on glass. Daguerrotype plates were on sale for the first time in France in 1839. In that year, too, Henry Fox Talbot, by obtaining photographic impressions from negatives, became the English inventor of photography as we know it. In 1841 Talbot was awarded a patent for producing Talbotype or Calotype prints on paper; in 1850 the Photographic Society of London was founded; and in 1851 collodion (solution of nitrated cotton in alcohol and ether) was applied to photography. In 1888 George Eastman was the first to introduce a roll of film into a hand-held camera, this being the greatest stimulus to amateur photography. There is no doubt that, from the 1840s onwards, artists were influenced to a greater or lesser extent by what still photographs were showing them.

[37]

Transverse gallop: horse fully extended
(Inset: *Ventre à terre*) (From *Reminiscences*)

Transverse gallop: legs flexed

Meanwhile, in 1881 the young American student of zoopraxography, Eadweard J. Muybridge, photographed, instantaneously, the movement of animals in rapid motion; but, as LE explained, that did not really give a true impression of speed. 'The advent of instantaneous photography has been both a boon and a curse to the artist,' he concluded. 'It has shown him the errors his forerunners committed in depicting movement, but it has bound him to a convention equally incorrect, since the motions depicted by the camera are not what we see, being a record of movement much too fast for the human eye to follow; yet he is compelled to use these instantaneous positions, because the public, seeing in the illustrated press nothing but these, will accept from the artist no imaginary action of his own. It follows that the artist must make the best of a bad job, and try to find what positions in instantaneous photography do suggest speed and ignore the rest. This is an art in itself, and I would refer the student to the chapter entitled "The Painter's Horse", in *Points of the Horse*, by Captain Mayes, F.R.C.V.S. He makes one statement which holds, to my idea, the whole art of depicting movement: "If both pair of limbs be depicted *sharply* in the canter or gallop, the chances are that the idea of motion will not be conveyed to the spectator." He goes on to say: "I can see no error of technique in giving indistinctness of outline to the limbs themselves; a painter who exhibited in the Royal Academy or Salon a picture representing a horse running away with a carriage would probably incur no rebuke from the art critics for blurring the spokes of the wheels, and drawing the legs and feet of the animal sharp, and yet those of us who know anything of the laws of motion must be aware that in such a case any one of the horse's feet going forward must be passing far faster through space

[38]

Rotatory gallop: dog fully extended   Rotatory gallop: legs flexed

than the more or less perpendicular spokes revolving through the lower half of the circle."

'Now let us take the indistinctness of outline. The style of the artist Malespino, whose racing pictures often appeared in the English press, is evidently founded on the above theory and is well worth the student's close attention. My own feeling is, that to give the impression of movement requires a lot of "wangling"! For example, if you can lose one foot in long grass, dust, snow, or in the background shadows, in fact, if by some means you can lose one of the four legs, as Hayes also suggests, you have already helped the illusion of speed.

'In depicting the gallop, if the horse can be shown reaching at its bit, the rider pulled well out of his saddle, it again helps. When the rider is galloping — really galloping, not cantering — leaning forward, either by crouching or standing in the stirrups, that too helps the illusion of speed. A modern horseman, rising at the jump, leans forward, goes with the horse — this suggests movement — but put him upright in his saddle — the way our fathers rode over fences — and it almost stops the horse pictorially. Bring him a little farther over the jump, commencing to land, tilt his body a little back, in the position assumed by all riders of the past, though only by a few of the present, and again you get the suggestion of movement. Curiously enough, if you put the rider right forward in landing, it doesn't appear correct, although this position is assumed by jockeys in a hurdle-race and all riders over a showjumping course.

'When you come to depicting more than one horse in movement your difficulties are more than halved and the more horses you can show galloping in the picture

[39]

the easier it is to give the illusion of speed. The innumerable legs – such a curse as a rule in a picture – in this case are a great help. If the horsemen can be slightly strung out, that is following each other without long gaps between them, and partially eclipsed by each other, so much the better. Leave gaps, especially if they are at regular intervals between the horses, and you destroy the illusion. The whole thing is very tricky, and wants far greater thought than we usually give to it. It is extraordinarily difficult to suggest racehorses coming straight at you and to keep the effect of pace – most photographs absolutely fail in this respect – but draw them going away from you in violent perspective, and no matter how bad a draughtsman you may be you can scarcely fail to get the effect of speed.

'Certain accessories are helpful in suggesting speed, for instance lines running in the same direction as the horses, but vertical lines such as telegraph-posts, trees, etc., have the opposite effect.

'The science of animal motion (zoopraxography) cannot be entirely ignored by artists, more especially since the advent of instantaneous photography has familiarised the public with the camera's version of animal movement – movements true in the slower motions but incorrect in rapid ones, being, as I have pointed out, too rapid for the human eye to see, and therefore producing grotesque positions which look as absurd as the conventional gallop of artists of the recent past.

'There are many dangers attached to the study of animal motion as recorded by

[40]

Impressions of speed:
Steeplechasing (From
'Crascredo's' *Horse
Sense and Sensibility*)

the camera, but the difference between walk, trot and rack, or pace, can well be studied. The gallop is full of pitfalls! I think that this pace is easiest understood if it is memorised that the horse has only one period of suspension (with all legs off the ground), i.e., when the animal's legs are all flexed (or gathered) under him. Therefore the legs stretched out fore and aft, as depicted by old-time artists, would only be correct if the animal depicted were a dog and not a horse. A horse in the extended position has always at least one leg on the ground, but there are two periods of suspension in the dog's gallop, one with all legs stretched out off the ground and the other with all legs gathered together (flexed) under him. This latter position is even then not quite similar to the same movement in the horse as owing to greater flexibility in the dog's backbone the legs cross each other, hind limbs on the outside. These two different ways of galloping are called in the horse the transverse gallop, in the dog the rotatory gallop. . . .'

[41]

During the Edwardian era LE was adding more to his knowledge of the chase, and his understanding of landscape art and of the portrayal of animal movement than at any other time of his career. The quality and appeal of his hunting pictures improved by the month – and, with that improvement, his income. Already he was receiving a steady stream of commissions from *Country Life, The Graphic, The Sphere* and other periodicals.

In 1909, he and Ethel let the Oxfordshire house and moved, in more civilised circumstances, to Worcestershire, where for the first time they employed a groom. He was not a success. 'He was . . . a young lad and a proper handful. He departed hastily after having ridden my second horse at the top of the hunt, so that, when I changed, the "fresh" horse was the more tired of the two!'

They hunted with the Croome, whose Master, Lord Charles Bentinck, also carried the horn and was considered by many of the pundits to be the best amateur of his day. LE remembers a frightening man with a harsh tongue, but one who ' . . . seldom gave offence. That charming lady his wife had, all the same, sometimes to smooth ruffled feathers. I well remember that famous sportsman, Tom Andrews, who had a slight stammer, saying *sotto voce* to Lady Charles, who was surrounded by a group of farmers, "Who be you b-b-buttering up today, milady? . . ."' Describing the big Croome coverts, with their boggy clay rides, LE goes on: 'When the field followed the huntsman into such places they were apt to hear about it! My wife, conscious that she was blocking up a narrow ride and hearing the Master (Lord Charles) coming, hastily pushed her horse down into the bushes below. "All right, all right, even if you are in the way you needn't commit suicide!" said the highly amused Master. . . .'

The Croome country was 'not ideal . . . having too many woods, market gardens and orchards', so after three seasons, the Edwardses, still accompanied by his mother, moved on to her home, Benarth, in north Wales. There, beyond the river flowing beneath the house, the country rose to the gorse and heather uplands. The horizon was the nearest point to Benarth hunted by foxhounds (the Flint and Denbigh), a riding distance of eight miles. 'This doesn't sound anything much' LE reminisces, 'but unfortunately it was the extreme boundary and not more than three or four times a season could I reach hounds in less than fifteen miles.

'Taken through the season the average hack each way worked out at sixteen miles – thirty-two miles in addition to the hunting! There were no motor horseboxes then, and need I say that no one else tried to do it in my district. But we were young then, though not our horses. Never before, or since, have I had horses as fit and

First Aid (From *Sketches in Stable and Kennel*)

well as these aged animals, thanks to H. Holloway, my groom. The long-distance road work kept them in a condition impossible to obtain in these days of motor horseboxes. The second-best fit horses I ever rode were two hirelings I once had, who had been running in a coach the previous summer, and came straight from that work into the hunting-field.

'Occasionally I drove myself to the more distant fixtures, taking my horse out of the shafts to hunt him. In the evening, after some warm gruel and a handful of hay, back he went into the shafts and trotted home. If he had gone lame we'd have had to stop the night out, but he never let me down – good old "Gay Lad"; his bones lie beneath the turf of Denbighshire.

'The Flint and Denbigh country is immense; it roughly stretches from the Dee to the Conway. They describe it in *Baily's Hunting Directory* as a bank and ditch country, comprising pasture and plough in fair proportions, "with some hill country". This description is so worded that it sounds as if they were far from proud of their hill country. In my opinion they are wrong because, unlike most of the hill countries that I know personally, their hills are rideable. You can get over the obstacles in the Denbighshire hills, but in most rough countries the walls are either too high to jump or the fences are entirely wire. The Flint and Denbigh country includes a nice vale, although the sea end of it is now spoiled. As a vale it has the disadvantage of being narrow, and foxes usually left it, and at the first opportunity returned to their beloved gorse-clad hills. Occasionally, however, a hill fox descended to the

Derby Day, 1913. On the occasion when Edwards and his agent, A. E. Johnson, hired a hansom cab for the big race. 'The old taxi in my sketch', he wrote in the 1930s, 'looks as out of date as the hansom'

43

The long, long summer day. Portman hounds in Kennel (From *Sketches in Stable and Kennel*)

vale, and then "fly fences" took the place of banks, and a sticky horse, unaccustomed to spreading himself, soon landed in the ditch which guards nearly all the vale fences. . . .

'I remember the astonishment of a holiday crowd at Rhyl when, having missed the train home after hunting, my wife and I, in wet and dirty hunting togs, came into dinner at one of the semi-fashionable hotels. It was, I remember, somewhere about 12 a.m. when we, and our tired horses, eventually got home that night – not that we often used the train as a covert hack, it was too expensive and much too unreliable. No wonder hunting people abandoned the railways in favour of the motor horseboxes. I remember a Welsh station-master saying in reply to my angry complaint at my horses having to wait for the next train: "Hunting peoples is no good to us, look you! A sovereign at Christmas and complaints twice a week is all they are good for!"

'Generally speaking, the marches of Wales, and most in fact of the less mountainous parts, are hunted by packs of crossbred English-Welsh hounds, such as the Bylffa, the Pantosgalog, etc.; but the Flint and Denbigh used pure-bred English hounds, and their hunt-servants were usually Englishmen. I always looked on both these as errors, but it cannot have really been so, or they would not have been carried on over so many years. To a stranger the peculiarity of hill hunting is the number of officials who carry horns. The system works well, as not infrequently the huntsman is at the bottom of a deep dingle, which takes ages to climb up, or go round, whilst the fox goes away at the top. In such cases the Master or the whip blows hounds away and goes on with them until overtaken by the huntsman – sometimes quite a long while after! It is, of course, extraordinarily easy to lose hounds anywhere, but particularly so in the hills. One day we caught hounds after losing them for half an hour or so, and I was amused at the remark of a visitor, who said, "Well, there's one thing to be said for this sort of 'unting. If after losing 'em for twenty minutes, and galloping wildly in the direction you think they've gone, it's darned satisfactory to find you've guessed right! . . .'

Those long hacks to the F and D country and days on the distant hills with their hounds were not enough to satisfy a man who was at once such a lover of venery and doggy person as LE. He needed a closer, more personal experience. So, opening up his father's old beagle kennels – which appear not to have been occupied for over twenty years – he put together a small pack of bloodhounds and cross-bred foxhound-bloodhounds. With those he hunted the 'clean boot', the quarry being a

Mountain Hunting. Watching the Ynsfor (From *Sketches in Stable and Kennel*)

man and the expression meaning that sporting bloodhounds work out their line from the man's general scent rather than from anything he carries or from the trace left by his feet.

The loose folds covering a bloodhound's skull, brow and jowl weigh down towards his muzzle when his head is lowered, to produce that extra nose capacity that renders him the most powerful, lowest scenting creature in the canine world. Bloodhounds are independent, jealous animals who do not work well together in a pack; so LE only kept a few couple of them. Because of the name 'bloodhound' he had some difficulty persuading locals that they were quite safe: 'People were afraid of these really remarkable gentle dogs. Apparently, stories of the slave trade, when Cuban bloodhounds were used for running down escaped slaves, have given the public the idea that these hounds are savage. I believe actually the Cuban variety is, having been crossed with mastiffs and other animals. Anyway the Cuban is not pure bred, which is the meaning of the word bloodhound – that is, "thoroughbred", like a "blood"

[46]

horse. Bloodhounds, I found, were arrant cowards, and the Welsh sheep-dog charging out frequently scattered the pack to the four winds. One of the funniest sights I have ever seen was my unfortunate hounds chased up the main street of a market town by a Pomeranian! . . . '

Another problem was that, as the hunting tradition in LE's part of Wales was tenuous and never well established he ran into quite a lot of trouble securing permission to ride across the land. On the other hand, having carefully pre-planned lines, there was no need to ride over crops or through sensitive coverts, so the damage was minimal. Hunting a man with very few hounds had the great advantage too, that ' . . . if you fall out with a landowner and he positively forbids you to ride over his land, there is little fear of your doing so unwittingly as most often happens when hunting a wild animal'.

LE's deep fascination with the mysteries of venery and scent and his determination to unravel them are further reflected in the notes he kept from the Bloodhound Hunt Club Open Field Trial Meeting, held in the Tedworth Country on November 26, 1913. I quote two entries. 'The first two hounds to be tried were Mrs Armitage's Weldbank Actor (dog) and Yeldham Coquette (bitch). The line was one hour 20 minutes cold. They found their man in 42 minutes. Scent was poor. Both hounds showed perseverance, and both found and identified their man . . . Mr Blomfield's Red Wrinkles found his man in 40 minutes, the line being one hour cold. This hound hunted in excellent style, never getting off the line, and throwing his tongue freely. He was hunted on foot, and the hound waited from time to time for his huntsman, which of course made the trial slow in point of time. With special training on colder lines this hound should be valuable for police work, his style of hunting being specially painstaking and sure. . . .'

If that doesn't show dedication to the study of hound-work how about this? 'Most of the hounds [at the field trial] ran *mute*. I have, however, often heard bloodhounds throw their tongues freely, notably at night. We once hunted by moonlight when there was a slight touch of frost, and it was very still — their voices echoing from far below, as they crossed one of the many wooded dingles, was one of the grandest sounds I have ever heard. It gave one a nasty feeling down one's spine and I was glad they were not hunting me! . . . Miss Guest [Elizabeth Augusta, then Master of "Miss Guest's", later of the Blackmore Vale] once hunted me with a doghound. I remember that, as I was being rapidly overtaken I climbed onto the roof of a cattle shed, and as he bayed, looking up with bloodshot eyes and hackles raised, for the

[47]

moment I forgot it was all in fun . . .' LE passed on his notes to H. M. Budgett, Master of the Bicester who made good use of them in his book, *Hunting by Scent.*

Being a very long way from the nearest town the Edwardses were obliged to be self-supporting, a condition that suited them well; for both being lovers of animals and of Nature they took readily to a farmer's life. Besides growing their own vegetables they kept cows and pigs and poultry and, for transport, a couple of carriage horses. One Jim Francis kept coach horses and coaches at Colwyn Bay and, through him LE maintained his close interest in that subject. But the Edwards's idyllic life of painting, farming, hunting and bringing up their children – Marjorie was born in 1908 and Derrick in 1910 – was halted abruptly, as it was for most other people, in 1914.

The looming war first impinged on their lives as they hacked to the last Flint and Denbigh meet of the 1913–14 season, which did not close until April. A long distance from home they encountered another horseman, consulting a map. The following dialogue ensued.

Stranger: 'I'm more or less lost. I'm looking for a farm called Ben Tyrion.'

LE: 'There is I think a farm of that name about two miles farther on the left, but I'm not very conversant with these parts myself. Also Bryn Tyrions are numerous.'

Stranger (having accompanied the Edwardses some distance and been told by LE that it was "a case of the blind leading the blind"): 'Are you going hunting?'

[48]

Over the Fence
(Watercolour)

Here's a health to every sportsman, be he stableman or lord!
(Pencil, watercolour and gouache)

The Marquess of Worcester (afterwards 10th Duke of Beaufort) hunting hounds, watched by his father the 9th Duke

The North Warwickshire going away from Skilts, 1924 (Pencil and watercolour, heightened with body colour)

The 1923 Grand National. Sergeant Murphy leading over Bechers, Captain Bennett up (Watercolour)

The South Atherstone running from High Cross towards Copstone (Watercolour)

Polo Ponies, India, 1927
(Watercolour)

LE: 'We are indeed.'

Stranger: 'I had no idea any pack hunted these wild hills.'

LE: 'Well, what on earth are you doing riding in them if you're not hunting your-self? Strangers are rare here, especially mounted ones.'

Stranger: 'I'm a Remount Officer, checking up on the horses on the farms with the official list of horses available in time of war.'

'It was', said LE 'the first vague hint of that great catastrophe which entirely changed the world as we knew it.' It was also his first introduction to the War Office department known as the Remount Service, the organisation which he himself would soon join – and serve for four years. A large number of middle-aged men had been appointed Remount Purchasing Officers with the task of procuring horses for the Yeomanry and other units; and now, with the war-clouds gathering more darkly, scores of nags were being congregated at all kinds of rendezvous. Classified as HD (heavy draught) LD (light draught gunners), R1 (cavalry) and R2 (smaller riding horses) these included racehorses and hunters (bought for a great deal less than half their value), crocks that had done nothing for years except trundle a light milk cart to the station, young unbroken horses, old farm horses near to breaking down and high-stepping cobs trained for the show-ring.

G. D. Armour. 'Unassuming Edwards gave GDA the accolade of being ". . . the only contemporary artist who really gets the winter atmosphere into his hunting scenes"'

G. D. Armour, Alfred Munnings and Cecil Aldin were already RPOs. 'It was terribly exciting,' GDA (who finished up a colonel) wrote in *Bridle and Brush*: 'and one felt there was something wrong with being left behind. Being fifty years old, I realised there was no front-line war glory for me. . . . All my friends were going or gone, I had to have some hand in it, however small. I heard that they wanted people to take some of the many horses they were landing from America to condition and put in order for use, so, having a number of open sheds, all facing south, and having a good deal to do with horses in the open I hung bails in the sheds, and got some thirty horses at once on applying. I beat up some grooms and young farm hands, and we soon had the animals coming on as well as possible considering they were pretty sick after the voyage and rough usage. We were paid twenty-five shillings per week for their keep and, at the price of fodder then, could do them well on it, labour included. I am sorry to say some unscrupulous people saw a chance of cheap money by turning the poor brutes out by hundreds on winter grass, but that was stopped when the remount officers had time to look round. . . .'

Aldin said that 'in buying horses in such haste, at the rate of ten or more an hour, with only the most superficial veterinary examination, there were in many cases a number of useless animals left on the Remount Depot's hands after a few weeks. I was called in by an inspecting officer during the first weeks of war to help in casting some of these which had been sent in from another section of the country, and on arrival I never saw such a marvellous collection of old-age pensioners and crocks collected in one yard. All horses as purchased had to be stabled and fed until issued, and as the very few regular remount depots in the country were filled immediately, purchasing officers were told to provide temporary stabling and staff for their purchases until they were wanted for issue. After the first few months and until new units were mobilised, those purchasing officers who were still kept on by the Remount Department had so many horses on their hands that the feeding, exercising and stabling became a big undertaking. At one time during the war on my daily inspection round I had to travel sixty miles, often having as many as five hundred horses under my temporary charge. Of these, almost daily issues to units of fit and suitable animals had to be selected, and constant batches of new puchases would be sent to these temporary depots to be stabled . . .'

As though the equine difficulties and frustrations were not serious enough the problems concerning staff were at least as bad. The remount soldiers were 'C3' men, unfit for active service. 'Even those,' remarks Aldin, 'becoming more and more rare', as the war took its toll and the medical standards for front-line troops were lowered.

LE was still at Benarth while all this work was getting under way. He remembers

[50]

strolling up to the paddock behind the stables with Ethel that August, to see the hunters at grass and, 'tempted by the glory of the westering sun, we continued our walk to a spot in the wood known as "the view". Here we sat and gazed seawards over Britannia's Realm.' Looking down towards the London–Holyhead railway they were suddenly dazzled by the flash of sun on metal. It was a sentry's bayonet. That was the first knowledge they had that war with Germany was a reality.

Old Mrs Edwards sold Benarth and went to live in London, while LE, 'having a large yet small family' (their third child Philip was born in 1914) and 'myself getting into the sere and sallow' (he was 36) 'pestered his friends' to find him a job with horses and duly joined the Remount Service. He was ordered to report to a depot in the south of England and was destined for 'four solid years of nothing but horse'.

The Remount Depot, Romsey, Hampshire, would be LE's wartime base. He and Ethel took a cottage at nearby West Wellow (in 1916 they moved to Manor Farm, East Wellow) where Ethel ran a smallholding, not only to feed her children but also because she loved caring for animals. Philip, died, a baby, in 1916, but Lindsay was born to them in 1917 and Kenneth in 1919. Although LE was obliged to live in camp he and Ethel would see one another most days of the week.

He arrived at the depot to find nothing more than a tin hut containing a staff sergeant, a couple of clerks and an 'extremely grumpy' adjutant who told him to 'clear out and wait until you're sent for!' Six weeks went by before that happened.

[51]

Most of the remount staff found life at the depot dull, but not LE for whom horses were 'a ceaseless interest'.

During the first few months, he says, the men were excellent – grooms, hunt servants, jockeys, stable lads and ex-cavalrymen. After a bit he is a little less enthusiastic, describing the Remount Service as 'a very mixed bag of both officers and men: old crusted cavalry officers and NCOs, with Masters of hounds, racehorse trainers, horse dealers, etc . . . the very different types mixed well but in the actual horse management frequently did not see eye to eye. . . .' Then he echoes Aldin: 'The continual medical boards whose job was to find replacements for the fighting units, eventually left us with a pretty mixed bag most of whom had never seen a horse before, and, I expect, never wanted to see another. It must have been a terrifying experience for, say, a bespectacled chemist's assistant to act as waiter at an equine meal, when he had to go in among unbroken animals, who at any rate had learned the meaning of the shouted order "feed!" and were kicking and squealing with excited anticipation.' Aldin's unit of girl grooms, on the other hand, was an unqualified success. ('Although many other remount establishments subsequently employed women', Aldin wrote proudly, 'I was the first to use women in this war work. At one period I had over one hundred ladies employed in my stables. I had very few failures . . .

Hunter Show,
Shrewsbury

my difficulty and the difficulty of my head woman being chiefly to watch that their "strappers" did not overwork and make themselves ill.)'

LE counted the mule as 'the most useful animal amongst His Majesty's four-footed soldiers', but went on to relate several instances (as G. D. Armour does in *Bridle and Brush*) of the strained and painful relationship between those tricky, if powerful, beasts of burden and the rag-bag conscripts who looked after them. 'Neither were together long enough to form friendships' he remarks with understatement, and goes on to quote a much travelled farrier-sergeant: 'Britishers an' mules don't click some'ow, yet I've seen them donkeys work like Christians for dagos and niggers and such-like.'

When G. D. Armour was asked by an inspecting general who tried out the prospective officers' chargers in his squadron, he replied that he did it. The general asked why he didn't delegate the job to the young subalterns. Armour explained that he didn't have any 'young subalterns', the united age of himself and his two assistant officers being 138 years. In the case of the three commissioned ranks at Captain Edwards's depot the aggregate age was 128. The commanding officer was well into his fifties, a fact mentioned by LE in the context of a story he tells about a certain Canadian mare. One day, after LE had classified an intake of remounts that had just arrived from Canada – one officer's charger, two cavalry troop horses, 58 light draught horses and six mules – the major commanding the depot asked to see the charger, which was a mare.

LE had the horse brought round to the squadron office, against the unyielding side of which the major was ejected the moment he got on her back. A rough-rider, who then attempted to mount her, was thrown so severely he had to be carted off to hospital. Several other experienced depot horsemen tried their hand but she defeated them all. Then some former cowboys from the depot's Canadian detachment asked LE if they could 'have a go with her' on a Sunday 'when the powers that be could be counted out of camp'. Accompanied by a crowd of spectators in Buffalo Bill costume, they arrived in stetsons, coloured shirts, chaps and spurs, and carried high-arched western saddles, quirts and ropes. They blindfolded the mare, roped her by a fore foot and a hind, cinched up the girths, then removed the blindfold, while one of their experts cautiously mounted her. They thought she was a buck-jumper, who would give the whole camp a rodeo display. They were wrong; she went straight up and backwards precisely as she had done with the others, tossing her rodeo rider unceremoniously from the saddle. 'Say Bill', he said to his mate while spitting out dust and gravel: 'd'you recognise this bitch? I guess we've met her before. 'Tis old

Calamity Jane, Canadian mare. 'Tossing her rodeo rider unceremoniously from the saddle' (From *Scarlet and Corduroy*)

Calamity Jane, who put us both on the floor at Calgary at last year's stampede!'

LE explained that 'she was as quiet as a sheep in stables, but had this one trick, which she had been encouraged to use; for apparently her only job had been to go the round of the shows performing it. . . . She was quite incorrigible, and in due course was cast as useless for military purposes. . . . I'm afraid the poor brute came to a bad end in civilian life from what I heard afterwards. She was last seen, a miserable wreck, pulling a station fly at a south coast station.'

LE tells us that 'the vast majority' of his charges were 'extremely coarse bred, common animals'. All the same it must have been extraordinarily sad for a man of his sentiments, who loved horses above all other creatures, to see either those or splendid animals that had been bred, broken and schooled by specialist equestrians and trainers for some particular performance – whether in the showring, over a steeplechase course, in the circus, on the farm, or in the hunting field – going into strange, rough stables, being tended by conscripts who knew little or nothing about the equine breeds. Then, perhaps, being cast as 'useless' for any war employment, and winding up in miserable circumstances such as that Canadian mare, who only reared because man had taught her to do it. Or worse still, probably, being sent to all the dreadful mud, shell and machine-gun and barbed wire hell of a First World War fighting front.

LE made the bitter comment after the war that the 377,312 horses and mules sent from the United Kingdom to France between 1914 and 1918 were 'completely forgotten'. As though to help pay the tribute that was owed, in 1918 he illustrated *The Horse in War*, by S. Galtrey, a work of much historical significance. It was, as Field Marshal Earl Haig wrote in the preface, 'a fleeting narrative of the vast and wonderful part played by our war horses, without which our armies of millions would have been immobile and impotent'.

LE frequently escorted consignments abroad during those four years, which he admits 'was a pleasant variation to everlasting stables, morning noon and night'. There must have been a mist in his eye as he saw his horses and mules from ferry to Continental goods van, and the railway guard raising the green flag that was the sign for them to make the next leg of their fateful journey — and out of LE's sight for ever. His Australian friend, Will H. Ogilvie, nearly all of whose collections of verse he illustrated, put it poignantly in his poem, *The Remount Train*:

> *Every head across the bar,*
> *Every blaze and snip and star,*
> *Every nervous twitching ear,*
> *Every soft eye filled with fear,*
> *Seeks a friend and seems to say:*
> *'Whither now, and where away?'*
> *Seeks a friend and seems to ask:*
> *'Where the goal and what the task?'*
>
> *Wave the green flag! Let them go! —*
> *Only horses? Yes, I know;*
> *But my heart goes down the line*
> *With them, and their grief is mine! —*
> *There goes honour, there goes faith,*
> *Down the way of dule and death,*
> *Hidden in the cloud that clings*
> *To the battle-wrath of kings!*

[55]

There goes timid childlike trust
To the burden and the dust!
Highborn courage, princely grace
To the peril it must face!
There go stoutness, strength, and speed
To be spent where none shall heed,
And great hearts to face their fate
In the clash of human hate!

Wave the flag, and let them go! —
Hats off to that wistful row
Of lean heads of brown and bay,
Black and chestnut, roan and grey!
Here's good luck in lands afar —
Snow-white streak, and blaze, and star!
May you find in those far lands
Kindly hearts and horsemen's hands!

Then giving a vision of the front line itself is Ogilvie's plucky little gunner horse in *The Offside Leader*, another to be depicted by LE:

She was a round-ribbed blaze-faced brown,
Shy as a country girl in town,
Scared of the gangway and scared of the quay,
Lathered in sweat at a sight of the sea,
But brave as a lion and strong as a bull,
With the mud at the hub in an uphill pull.
She learned her job as the best ones do,
And we hadn't been over a week or two
Before she would stand like a rooted oak
While the bullets whined and the shrapnel broke,
And a mile of the ridges rocked in glee,
As the shells went over from Battery B.

My mates have gone and left me alone;
Their horses are heaps of ashes and bone.
Of all that went out in courage and speed
There is left but the little brown mare in the lead,
The little brown mare with the blaze on her face
That would die of shame at a slack in her trace,
That would swing the team to the least command,
That would charge a house at the slap of my hand,
That would turn from a shell to nuzzle my knee —
The pride and the wonder of Battery B. . . .

Both Lionel and Ethel were well served by his batmen, of which, being in a draft-finding unit, he had quite a succession, all of whom, apparently, were perfectly willing to work on the farms and gardens at the Wellows. When Ethel offered to pay Private Flynn, a soldier of Irish-Scottish parentage, the man replied, 'Can I no dig for me 'ain pleasure?' On one occasion Lionel's brother, Brigadier-General Fitz, was staying with them on leave and helping with the hay harvest. Fitz and Lionel made the mistake of stacking some hay wet. Flynn, seeing it becoming hot and steamy, grumbled about it under his breath. 'Why don't you tell them?' asked Ethel. 'An' is it for me to tell a general what to do?' replied Flynn. At the depot one day LE found another soldier-

[57]

servant who had been assigned to him, sitting on the end of his (Edwards's) bed, thumbing through his sketchbooks. The man, who had been huntsman to the Brocklesby, was taken completely by surprise. He jumped to his feet with this explanation: 'Many apologies, sir, but your sketches are the only bit of hunting I ever see these days.' It was a long time since Captain Edwards had felt such sympathy for a conscript.

He is continuously diffident about his wartime service. 'Being a very amateur soldier I failed to cadge much leave, but was lucky now and again to get a day with the Duke's, then being hunted by a brother officer, Captain Herbert Nell. . . .' He stressed, in strong terms, that the Remount Service would have been much better run on a civilian basis. ('There was a great wastage of manpower in guards, drills, etc, which could have been far better employed in stables'.) The memory of attending a military crammer thirty years before would have brought a cynical smile to his lips. 'Being by nature no soldier, no one was more glad to be demobbed than I was.'

LE's impression of an incident in the history of the Coldstream Guards. Lt-Col Jock Campbell VC, Master of the Tanatside Foxhounds, rallies his battalion with a hunting horn to lead a decisive counter-attack on the Somme, in 1916 (From *Sport in War*)

III

THE GREAT NIMROD-PAINTER

THE DUSK IS DOWN

The dusk is down on the river meadows,
The moon is climbing above the fir,
The lane is crowded with creeping shadows,
The gorse is only a distant blur.
The last of the light is almost gone,
But hark! They're running!
They're running on!

The count of the years is steadily growing;
The Old give way to the eager Young;
Far on the hill is the horn still blowing,
Far on the steep are the hounds still strung.
Good men follow the good men gone;
And hark! They're running!
They're running on!

Will H. Ogilvie

The Quorn at Shoby cross-roads. (From *My Hunting Sketch Book*, Vol. 2)

'From this period I started on a more serious and strenous effort to make a living out of sporting art', LE wrote of the post-war era; 'and visited more packs than I can remember in the next twenty years.' Through wartime's force of circumstances his travels to the hunt countries during the remainder of his long life were to be from a base at the extreme south of England. Ethel and Lionel had made their home near Romsey, close to LE's remount depot; and the Hampshire coast was to be their lifelong environment. The second season after the Armistice he was riding with the Hursley hounds when he spotted a Victorian house — with a yellow-brick facing, twelve miles from Salisbury on the Hampshire Downs, upon which he set his heart.

Enquiries revealed that the property was called Buckholt and was part of the Norman Court estate belonging to Washington Singer of the American sewing machine family (himself, incidentally, a hunting man: he had been Master of the South Devon at the turn of the century). The agents told LE the house was to let. The Edwardses needed a larger place — the birth of Lindsay in 1917 and Kenneth in 1919 brought their score of children up to four. Buckholt contained twelve bedrooms. They rented the property — complete with substantial stabling and a small farming estate — from 1921 until 1945 when Singer died and they were able to buy it. Having purchased horses from the Army, LE had already established stables at Romsey. It was a great relief to be able to move them to the larger accommodation.

Like his father — and Ethel, too — he had always been preoccupied with soil and stock. And ' . . . as I have always believed it to be a terrible mistake, for an artist especially, to put all his eggs in one basket, I gradually started farming more seriously. . . . Moreover I have always looked upon it as the most satisfactory, although by no means the most profitable, of trades.'

When people said they couldn't understand why, as a hunting artist, he didn't live in the Midlands his reply was: 'If I lived in a good hunting country the temptation to hunt would be so great that I should do no painting. Secondly, the expenses would be too great for any artist's pocket. By living in less fashionable districts rent and rates, wages and horses' keep are at least halved, and, after all, hunting only takes place six months in the year, and for the other six I prefer to live in a good hacking country, and also (again from an artist's point of view) the provinces are far more picturesque than the Shires.'

The war made as much of a break in his life as it did in anyone's. It not only moved him from north Wales to south Hampshire, but from 1914 onwards he saw little of his then London-based mother, to whom he had been so close (she died

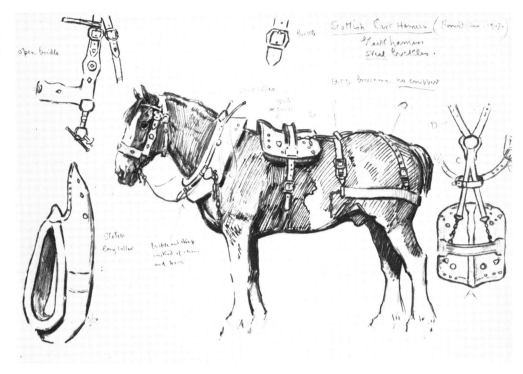

Scottish cart harness.
(From *Thy Servant the Horse*)

in 1916). He was largely separated in those four years, too, from his craft and creativity. With the help of his good agent, A. E. Johnson, of Kingsway, London, LE had staged his first one-man exhibition in the summer of 1914 at Graves's Gallery, in Pall Mall, and throughout the War he was sending in articles and sketches to *Country Life*; but he had to leave painting virtually behind for the duration. Yet 'curiously enough' – he echoes Cecil Aldin – 'this abstinence from the use of brush, pen and pencil, seemed to have freshened my outlook . . . pre-war and post-war mark definite periods and in my case rather different classes of work.'

What was the future of hunting? In 1919 sportsmen were as sceptical as Regency men had been with the burgeoning of canals; as the early Victorians were when the railways drove their ugly tracks through the countryside; or as the Edwardians when the farmland began to be seriously criss-crossed with barbed wire. 'My father, who hunted with the Cheshire in the 1850s, told me as a small boy (in reply to my demands for a pony)', Lionel remembered, 'that he did not think hunting, at any rate in Cheshire, would last through my time – so why learn to ride?' Apart from the fact that the war had stolen a heavy toll of young men who might have taken on Masterships or become hunt servants, many of the big estates had been – or

[62]

Partridge shooting

were about to be – broken up; and by no means all the owner-occupiers and small-holders would want the hunts trampling over their precious plots. Cars had replaced draught horses, grooms had become mechanics; and the social and economic revolution caused by the upheaval of the holocaust had generally smeared the image of old Edwardian England. Jack was as good as his master, while the new taxation rendered his master rather short of money.

Notwithstanding those problems optimism soon reigned in the countryside. LE was out with the Hursley in March, 1919, his first day's hunting in civilian clothes after the war. There being snow on the ground and no scent – he records in the second volume of *My Hunting Sketch Books* – he described the conditions as 'putrid' to a friend. 'Seeing hounds and a pink coat are sufficient for me,' replied the fellow-sportsman. 'I never expected to see either again, did you?'

1919 found LE started on the venatic excursions that were to bring him such fame. 'My mother loved motoring,' says their daughter, Marjorie. 'However long the journey she never seemed to tire. They were completely fearless motorists and liked travelling very fast. That was usually necessary because LE insisted on taking "short cuts" which were inclined to double the length of the journey!... Neither of them

[63]

Mrs Inge, MFH. 'She was such a charming personality' said LE, 'that everyone took care not to incur her displeasure'

drove. My father hired from a Mr Dawkins, who acted as chauffeur. Towards the end of the 1930s they engaged a man of their own, Rogers. They always had Austins, nothing else would do. . . .' The excellent Rogers served the Edwardses until 1939 when he was called up.

LE was not the first artist to travel the hunting countries. John Ferneley had tried it; in the 1890s G. D. Giles did a series of colour plates of the most fashionable hunts, and Cecil Aldin had got a sizeable set together; but there would be never anything to beat Lionel Edwards's pictorial record of British and Irish hunting. It would be much larger and more comprehensive, it would hold substantially more appeal than the others – and above all, express far greater seasonal, regional and sporting eloquence and incisive truth.

He began in the Midlands, in the autumn of 1919, with the Atherstone, which would remain his favourite country throughout his career. It was an excellent one to launch forth with, for there was not a hunt in Britain with higher buoyancy and morale. Mrs Inge, the widow of an Edwardian Master, had succeeded Norman Loder (immortalised as Denis Milden in Sassoon's *Memoirs of a Foxhunting Man*) in 1914. At the time of LE's visit she was in her last season, with the great Sam Morgan as huntsman and Jack Molyneux, who was to be equally famous, as 1st whipper-in. In his admiration for Mrs Inge, LE wrote: 'I was immensely impressed by her command

Mrs H. G. Gregson, MFH, 1960

Mares and Foals at Clanville Farm (Canvas)

Tandem Dog Cart
(Watercolour on buff
paper)

*Ireland – Nothing Stops
'Em!* (Watercolour)

Mrs Denis Aldridge as
Edwards first knew her on
Exmoor in the 1920s

over her field: nowhere before or since have I seen a hard-riding field so well behaved,
yet less "dragooned". The reason for this marvellous discipline can be summed up
by saying that even in her old age she always went first over every kind of obstacle,
for as is well known a hard-riding field can only be properly controlled from in front.
Besides, she was such a charming personality that everyone took care not to incur
her displeasure. They told me that, although she never drilled her field, her upraised
hand was sufficient to stop even the wildest thrusters, and that should anyone ignore
this signal to hold hard, she would ask a friend of the culprit to convey her mild
rebuke.'

In 1930 the Atherstone country was reconstituted with kennels to cater for both
the north and the south ends. It was there on the Leicestershire–Warwickshire border
that LE first stayed with Kathleen and Denis Aldridge, whom he had met on Exmoor
and who were to become his and Ethel's closest friends. Aldridge was wire secretary
to the South Atherstone, and also quite a promising artist. Naturally he took every
opportunity offered to snatch a lesson off the great master. 'I can show you most
insights I've had in painting hunting scenes', LE told him in Mrs Aldridge's hearing;
'and I can tell you what to look for in capturing the individual characteristics of
horses and hounds. . . . But not people. I'm no good at facial likenesses.' He did himself
less than justice, for although he was never as good at portraiture as some of his

fellow sporting artists (notably Armour and Haigh), he often achieved a very fair one; and, what was really just as clever, he nearly always captured the individual's riding seat and style. Kathleen Aldridge thinks one of the best likenesses he ever achieved was that of her husband, dressed and mounted for a day's hunting. She emphasises the terrific speed at which he painted. Her husband could never keep up. LE always made a point of putting the sky down first – before it changed. 'Get that sky, Denis!' he'd say 'Quick, quick. . . . There, now you've lost it!' His dramatic wintry skies became celebrated far beyond the hunting world; a Poet Laureate would immortalise them. Here's Betjeman in *Hertfordshire*:

> *I had forgotten Hertfordshire*
> *The large unwelcome fields of roots*
> *Where, with my knickerbockered sire*
> *I trudged in syndicated shoots;*
>
> *And that unlucky day when I*
> *Fired by mistake into the ground*
> *Under a Lionel Edwards sky,*
> *And felt disapprobation round . . .*

'Lionel was a tall, distinguished, rather military-looking man' – Mrs Aldridge sang his praises to me – 'with the most beautiful manners and a lovely sense of the ridiculous. He absolutely adored his wife, you know, and invariably took her advice over his painting and over most other things, too. He was charming with children and always listened very courteously to what they had to say. He never interrupted them. And, of course, they loved him, too, though he was a quiet man, reserved and sometimes forbidding. He didn't suffer fools gladly. . . .'

Unassuming Edwards gave G. D. Armour the accolade of being ' . . . the only contemporary artist who really gets the correct winter atmosphere into his hunting scenes. For it *is* winter. It rains and blows and men and horses sweat and get covered in mud in his pictures exactly as they do in the real thing. The blue skies and satin-skinned horses of summer do not enter into his views of the chase. . . .' But LE himself is the one who is really remembered for that, because he succeeded better than all the other (really good) sporting artists in making everything in his hunting scenes come together in one whole feeling of clay-spattered, yet enormously elegant, combination of brave high-spirited sportsmen and women and strong, lithe, well-bred horses and hounds, each a character of its own, in an ambience of leafless trees, wet pastures, deep ploughs, flooded lanes and menacing skies — whether at covertside, going to the draw, at the find, casting or going back to kennels.

'What is the magical charm of the Shires?' he asks. 'It can be summed up in one word — Grass. Yet there are many parts of the country full of old pastures, such as the Blackmore Vale, etc. But Leicestershire grass rides light in comparison, and although the rolling ridge and furrow tires horses unaccustomed to the country, the going is always good . . . making the big fences of the Pytchley and Fernie country far less formidable than they appear.' Soon after the Atherstone he took his first day with the Shires' premier pack, the Quorn — in their moorland (Charnwood Forest) country — where his abiding impression was of 'Walter Wilson, their famous huntsman, sitting silent and aloof on his horse, surrounded by his hounds. What was so remarkable was that every hound had his or her eyes on Wilson; he had, all the time, and apparently without effort, got their undivided attention. It was the perfect human and canine fox-catching machine. . . .'

Walter Wilson, Huntsman to the Quorn, showing at Peterborough. 'He had all the time, and apparently without effort got his hounds' undivided attention' (From *Huntsmen Past and Present*)

[67]

Frank Freeman, Huntsman to the Pytchley. 'It is really an education to watch this master of the science hunt hounds' (From *Huntsmen Past and Present*)

[68]

The Masters were Major Algy Burnaby and A. E. Paget, 'a great combination'. He found Burnaby 'the most delightful character' and laughed long and loud to hear him shout to the field, 'Look out, look out! Loose horse coming with a lady on it!' on losing his patience with a woman who had little control of her mount. On another occasion when a hard-riding Diana jumped in among the sacrosanct Quorn hounds, according to LE, Burnaby burst out: 'Will no one stop that bitch?' adding, just in time, 'she's getting in the way of the riders!'

He pays due credit to the refreshing lead given by the Prince of Wales (Edward VIII) to the hunting world in the post-war years, and looks back on a speech 'full of the enthusiasm of youth', given by the Prince to the Quorn farmers at Leicester in 1925: 'I wish to say "thank you", not as Prince of Wales but as a hunting man. I am very grateful to all connected with hunting in this country who have made it possible for me to enjoy the wonderful sport I have had for the last four seasons. . . .'

LE was privileged to go out with the Pytchley when Frank Freeman – thought by many to be as brilliant as Tom Firr – carried the horn, and sketched a view looking from near Guisborough towards Cottesbrook, commenting that 'even the flower of Weedon had their work cut out to keep up with that wonderful old huntsman . . . for those who love hunting it is really an education to watch this master of the science hunt hounds'. His next painting of Freeman was to be in 1931, in the huntsman's last season, watched in action by 5-year-old Princess Elizabeth on her pony accompanied by her mother, the Queen. In another Pytchley scene LE was lucky enough to get the giant airship, the R101, into his picture, hovering over Tally-Ho gorse as members of the field were hacking home. Of all five Shire packs the Pytchley earned his warmest affection.

Choosing 'a beautiful bit of grass looking towards Whissendine' he depicted the Cottesmore from a find at the legendary Ranksboro' gorse. Then Dawkins drove him on to the Fernie for which he had a special fondness 'entirely because, as an occasional visitor, I was always lucky in my day and mount'. He had a hireling for a Belvoir opening meet and wrote in his diary: 'A good hunt from Sproxton Thorns, of which I saw little being frightened of both crowd and fences.' He was rather unimpressed by the grandeur of the Shires. 'As a casual and impecunious visitor one saw little of the so-called Melton set. They seemed to me very ordinary people, although rather jealous of strangers, perhaps.'

Dawkins and the faithful Austin took him on to the Warwickshire where he positioned himself with a pleasant view of Edgehill, sketched the fox turning just in front

of him and the pack in full cry half a field behind. They went to Badminton to make a picture of the old Duke of Beaufort rugged up with a terrier on his knees, chauffeur-driven while his son and heir, Lieutenant the Marquess of Worcester, Royal Horse Guards, soon to be 10th Duke, doubles his horn in a gateway. Gone Away! He painted the South Staffordshire with hounds crowding through a gap in a stake-and-bound and the huntsman and his horse standing quietly at the check, enshrouded in perspiration.

In a study of the Whaddon Chase he shows a riderless grey nearest to his canvas, which looks down from the Aylesbury–Buckingham road towards the galloping scarlet and black and over the Denham hills towards the Bicester country with an overcast sky tinted with pink and purple. Some of the pictures were painted from the Austin, which ' . . . being very light, even if it does subside into the clay ruts of a muddy lane', he explains, 'can usually be easily extricated. . . . Under less luxurious circumstances (that is in those numerous places to which a mechanical vehicle cannot take one) I'm afraid the viewpoint has, on several occasions, been determined by the direction of the wind and the proximity of a hedge as a windscreen, since it

[70]

Beyond Court Hall, North Molton, Devon. Painting the Hon. Sheila Bampfylde, daughter of Lord Poltimore

is quite impossible to keep up a sketching easel on a really windy day. . . .'

On they go from country to country, returning intermittently to Hampshire and their beloved Buckholt and their four children and the piling letter-box with its ever-increasing commissions and requests. The Buckholt studio afforded scarcely more comfort than the Austin. Visitors wore overcoats and scarves. LE disdained stoves, electric fires or any other form of heating. Nor did he shiver.

The first volume of his *Hunting Sketch Books* was out in 1928. On the title page of Volume II, which was published two years later, he quotes a versifier in the *Sporting Magazine* of 1822:

> *I like the sketch — one of its charms is this:*
> *You may correct it should it be amiss;*
> *A finished picture is another thing,*
> *And must be left to fate and its own colouring.*

The colours frequently still lay wet on his canvas when he set off again now with Dawkins and a tall shooting brake, an Austin Traveller, with his easel all ready to be set up between the back doors. Perhaps his most cherished 'Provinces' (as distinct from 'Shires') were in the West Country and, above all, Exmoor which was why he was so good at drawing and painting deer in their environment. (Many critics

[71]

hailed him as the best ever in that sphere.) The moors drew him towards themselves as though magnetically. He had followed up his pre-war Devon visits with more excursions in the 1920s. On one of those he stayed with Lord and Lady Poltimore, at Court Hall, North Molton, to paint their children, John and Sheila Bampfylde, a photograph of him in that act being shown in these pages. Sheila Bampfylde (since 1932, the Hon. Lady Stucley, of Hartland Abbey, Bideford), told me that she remembers ' . . . a most charming man, shy and unassuming, but always very kindly and cheerful'. She repeats Mrs Aldridge's verdict that 'he was brilliant at animal likenesses but not much good at human faces'.

To portray the Devon and Somerset Staghounds he stood on Stoke Ridge ' . . . which I abandoned for my *Shires and Provinces* series in favour of Cloutsham, which is so much better known, although Stoke Ridge is not much more than a mile farther on. Looking from the Exford road across Stoke Ridge, Wilmersham, Porlock hill and Vale, one gets, I think, quite the pick of the scenery in this part of the West Country.'

The loneliest Dartmoor valley imaginable and the grey stone pile of Tor Eagle Rock provide the setting for his South Devon Foxhounds scene, while on the side of the picture he recalls the local saying: 'On Exmoor you can ride anywhere, except where you can't; on Dartmoor you can't ride anywhere except where you can!' Then Austin, Dawkins and artist proceed to Cornwall for a presentation portrait of the Master of the Four Burrow, that great amateur huntsman and breeder of hounds, Percival Williams, LE observing that: 'The inhabitants of these parts are largely tin miners and smallholders, keen sportsmen and puppy walkers to a man. A considerable number of them, apart from those who ride, hunt on foot, armed with field-glasses. They betake themselves to the high ground and watch with the greatest enthusiasm the performances of their particular "dogs".' Journeying east he visits two or three of the Dorset hunts. And now he is ready for Buckholt again.

As his two books *The Wiles of the Fox* and *The Fox* show, he made quite a study of the natural history of that quarry, its scent, movements, diet, and mating and breeding habits and how it eludes the mighty pack. He once kept a fox as a pet for several years and, like all good foxhunters had little interest in seeing Reynard killed. He says as much in *My Hunting Sketch Books*, and goes on to state that 'it is the accessories of the chase that constitute its charm. . . . Not the least of them is the beauty of the landscape (to say nothing of the variety of obstacles which the follower of the chase rides over). It is most unsafe to generalize on any subject, but my own view is that the pick of our hunting countries (from a riding point of view) are *not* the

[72]

most picturesque. Therefore the artist and sportsman are ever at war within me. If I were required to say as an artist where I had seen the most beautiful hunting scenes, I would reply: With the Linlithgow and Stirling hounds on the banks of the Forth, with the Fife Hills in the distance; or with the Flint and Denbigh hounds in their hill country behind Coed Coch, looking towards the snow-capped Caernarvonshire mountains; or with the same pack in Flintshire, looking across the mouth of the Dee to the Wirral peninsula. But, from a riding point of view, I am bound to confess "the finest view in Europe" *is* to be found within fifteen miles of Melton. . . . Last, but not least, there are the charming vagaries of the English weather! For even our pale and wintry sunlight can turn the most sodden, uninspiring plough country into a dream of fairyland.'

Everything up to date in the studio, Austin Traveller packed, it's north again towards the Midlands now for a portrait of the South Notts pointing over the River Trent (which, notes the diary, 'fox crossed and escaped'). Then another Quorn visit, followed by Yorkshire and the Bedale for one of those difficult scenes 'which, when one tries to fit figures into it one is bound to admit defeat'. (Yet the result is another

[73]

marvellous hunting landscape!) Co. Durham next and the Zetland with which his most striking memory is of Raby Castle: ('Apart from being the most picturesque inhabited castle I have ever seen the carriage drive into the house intrigued me immensely'). Then the Duke of Buccleuch's, the great open moorland of Roxburghshire and Berwickshire and stone walls and hovering mauve clouds leading the eye down to the main point of action.

May, 1925, sees him in London for the opening of another exhibition of his pictures set up for him by the faithful A. E. Johnson at the Sporting Gallery, 32, King Street, Covent Garden. Gerald S. Davies, the Master of Charterhouse, wrote it up in *Country Life*. 'There is a test' he said, 'which the average man sometimes puts to out-of-door paintings: Do they give you the sense of the open air? Do they make you see the moving sky and feel the breeze in your face and scent the crushed grass and the ploughed earth and the growing woodland? A good test, I venture to think, though not, of course, the only test. . . . And yet I am well aware that the highbrows of criticism would regard it as puerile, and will have none of it. It is too natural, too free from the jargon of art, too much of an appeal to the uninstructed in art. Never mind. Even from their point of view it should be highly considered, since it represents in effect an "impression" of a very real kind. It is a great asset, and one which even the greatest landscape painters have often not possessed, though they have possessed many others. And this quality may be claimed in the highest degree for Mr Lionel Edwards's hunting pictures.

'If you have any doubts, go and listen – it is lawful listening – to the criticisms of the men and women who evidently derive sheer delight from the subjects (unconscious of their sin against the canon of highbrows) and the way in which they are made to yield their full stock of fresh and delicious memories. "I'll bet you he enjoyed doing that", said a girl to her husband. "Oh, say, don't you want to be there!" and the like.

'So much for the fresh atmosphere which is borne in upon one from these pictures. But there are other assets besides. Mr Edwards is a great artist, even, I should imagine to the visitor who never sat astride a saddle. Mr Edwards is a colourist – within the limits, *bien entendu*, which he has set himself. Hunting is a winter sport when mainly the skies are grey, when the landscape, even in the heathery moors of Devonshire, is of low tone. And how he knows the secret of the little bit of pink coat in bringing out the value of this greyness!

'I should name No. 28 "The Challenge" as the high water of Mr Lionel Edwards's

Self-Portrait with son Ken, 1925

achievement: a work good enough to go into one of the National collections. . . .
This "Challenge" may be ranked with the work of a great artist, Sir Edwin Landseer,
now as undeservedly under-rated as he was once foolishly over-praised.'

'Mr Lionel Edwards possesses a quality which possibly escapes most of those who
admire his works' wrote another critic. 'He can be called a landscape painter first
and a sportsman-painter afterwards. He is one of the artists – how few they are
– who realise that the soul of a sporting picture is its setting. I would dare wager
that it can be truly said of him that he has never painted a landscape which he has
not seen: wherein he is very different from the majority. You could lift horses, hounds
or any other animate figure you please, out of any of his paintings and still leave
a complete landscape and a real picture.'

The art of pursuing the hare on foot fascinated LE as much as hunting the fox
by horse. Nor was beagling a branch of venery in which he welcomed his concentra-
tion on the subject being interrupted any more than he did during a foxhunt – as
he pointed out in *Scarlet and Corduroy.* There he complained of 'an old lady who
took the opportunity at a check to discuss Poor Law problems – of all moments
surely the most inopportune, for in beagling a check is the most exciting and most
crucial time. The mind is debating the probable run of the hare; the eyes shift from
hound to hound as they spread fanwise o'er the field, watching for that little extra

[75]

Ireland in the '20s. Lionel and Ethel at the mercy of a drunken driver. '"Indade" (LE quotes him) "an' she's a great little pony" – whack! whack!' (From *Scarlet and Corduroy*)

wagging of a stern that shall proclaim a line. Great Diana! Fancy thinking of Poor Law problems! I agreed with Beckford, who said that "amongst the ancients it was thought an ill-omen to speak out hunting".'

But he revelled in back-chat and amusing impudence in the hunting-field and stored up a splendid fund of stories for posterity. He enjoyed hearing a fellow-sportsman tell a pompously excited admiral to 'shut up and go back to your blinkin' old barge!' He had another good laugh when a certain Master described how, on offering his second horseman a pull on his flask, the man drank it to the last drop. When the MFH remonstrated the man replied: 'Well, sir, the trouble was I couldn't get at my share without drinkin' yours first!' And he remembers a less engaging Master in the West Country who lost his temper with an old shepherd who blocked a gateway with his flock and was in no hurry to move on. 'Now look 'ere, zur! Let me tell 'ee some 'ut', retorted the shepherd. 'If you was 'arf as free with yourn 'arf crowns as you be with yourn tongue, 'untin' would be a deal more pop'lar in these parts!'

As a devoted hunting man LE was bound to reserve a special place in his heart for Ireland, to feel the adrenalin going as he crossed choppy St George's channel for one of his many Irish tours. His first expedition was soon after 'the Troubles'

when the people were still inclined to be dour and suspicious; blown bridges were
not repaired, cars made precarious journeys over temporary wooden structures; the
drab grey towns were at their most drab from sheer poverty; the green pillar-boxes
thinly disguised the bright red of Queen Victoria's postal services and the VR inscrip-
tions; deserted houses gave the landscape a forlorn air; and, from habit, the Anglo-
Irish moved about in some trepidation. (He relates an occasion on which his hostess
was driving him to a meet, when 'suddenly, coming round a corner and under a
railway arch we almost ran into a band of idlers. She crashed the brakes on. "What's
the trouble?" I asked. "Just that, momentarily I thought we were back in it", she
replied. "I'm sorry I lost my nerve. Let's get on, we're late".'

As a sporting visitor to Ireland he applauded the lack of ploughland and of wire,
the scarcity of roads, the absence of urban development, the small 'fields' and the
warm hospitality (as indeed we do in the 1980s); he noted with pleasure that 'hontin''
owned a more integral place in the countryside than it does in England and he wrote
with warm fellow-feeling about the men of the trencher-fed harrier packs who met
on Sundays (but never before attendance at Mass). As an artist he basked in the
warm moist climate of sunlight and shadow, the uniquely vivid green of the pastures,

[77]

Razor-top bank, Ireland. How not to do it! (From My Irish Sketch Book)

the purple of the mountains, the dazzling blue of the streams and gold of the gorse. 'Our first draw is a little humped-up rocky gorse in the midst of some boggy fields', says a diary note. 'Across these the gulls come flying from the sea to skim by without a sound, while from the rushy pastures the snipe go flickering away in front of hounds as the latter move off to draw.'

He loved the spirit and even the hazards of Irish hunting, the thrill of the banks and ditches and doubles, as this passage from one of his descriptions well shows. '. . . Then followed a succession of easy banks, all downhill, to another river bank, where hounds threw up. They were cast over the shallow river by their huntsman, and picked up the line, hunting slowly to ground in a bank. We then drew a rushy pasture in which were patches of whin, and found again. Evidently we were in for a hunt this time, for suddenly the field started to "go". Personally I thought this (and most Irish fields) somewhat alarming. They certainly *all* have a go, and not merely 15 per cent as in England, but as so many ride young horses (for sale) in snaffle bridles, over which they have little control, their proximity is sometimes alarming, and if perchance you have for the moment got a front seat in the stalls, it gives you a nasty feel in your back if your horse makes the slightest error!

'Yet I don't think horses fall so often in Ireland. Possibly it is because big banks

[78]

are obstacles which reduce the speed of all concerned (including the fox). All the same an "error in dimensions" gives you a nasty fall at a bank, or a very wet one at a Meath ditch. At the latter, fortunately, a "wrecker" usually appears like magic, and after lengthy bargaining, proceeds to draw your engulfed horse out, like a cork from a bottle! These onlookers are usually herdsmen and well deserve the tips they get. All the same, quite a few, I fancy, are not quite the genuine article, and sometimes one found a figure standing in the only jumpable place, who said, "An' will I knock the gap, yer honor?", but unless your hand goes pocketwards he does not unduly hurry to do so.'

The character and ambience of it all is well and truly distilled into *My Irish Sketch Book* with studies of the Muskerry heading back to kennels in a rain-laden gale while the huntsman blows for lost hounds; the Limerick, led by John Alexander MFH, going buoyantly away from Garryfine with the Galtee mountains for a backcloth; a scarlet-coated follower hazarding his top hat through a bank's overgrowth with the Carlow; the Kilkenny galloping through heavy grass at Castle Morris; the Kilkenny again hard on their fox's brush on the rock of Kilteely; and, again, crossing the road in and out of stone walls, watched by an old woman in a donkey cart; the Ward Union riders making their cavalry charge at the first bank the moment their stag has a suitable lead; the Meath hounds hard on a line at Tara; and the Waterford – painted for Lady Waterford when James Russell was Master and huntsman; and many humorous sketches aptly captioned.

'One forgot the buffeting of the Irish channel, the slow, cold journey by train in the early morning and the fact that there was no car to meet one on arrival, mine hostess having forgotten the time whilst shopping. . . . Forgotten are all past discomforts; for tomorrow we hunt, and for the present we sit down to a real tea, eggs and bacon, potato cakes and hot tea (laced with whiskey – mine host has been hunting, whilst I have the excuse of having travelled far). Of course the talk is of hunting, hounds and horses and what shall *he* ride tomorrow. . . . There is no doubt that Irish hunting has a potent charm. What fun it all is!'

Now London again and the Sporting Gallery where the pictures he painted for Will Ogilvie's *Over the Grass* are on view, about which another *Country Life* writer, 'Crascredo' eulogises: 'I was reading a book, when from it there fluttered down an invitation to go right across the world with Mr Ogilvie and Mr Lionel Edwards, all among men and horses; and, at the last, to turn again – and "ride the English grass". The book was Mr Ogilvie's *Over the Grass* which Messrs Constable have

[79]

recently published, with Mr Lionel Edwards's illustrations in colour. The world which I was invited to cross was that of the Sporting Gallery's latest exhibition where, with many other most attractive pictures, are the originals of the illustrations to Mr Ogilvie's poems. I went. And I have just come back. It has been equal to all expectations.

'I first walked into Mr Lionel Edwards's stable-yard with Mr Ogilvie: a stable-yard at exercise time when the snow is on the ground, when—

> *Clicking their snaffles the hunters pass*
> *Round in the straw-laid ring.*

'It was obvious at once that this was the real thing. Nobody but nature and Mr Lionel Edwards can get that blue light on the snow. . . . I have told you before now and I daresay you have told me just what it is about Mr Lionel Edwards's horses and hounds which sets us all agog and agoggle; but have you ever considered why it is that none of his hunting pictures seems to be a picture at all? It is because he does not *show* you a picture: he shows you this very England, all stretched out before you – seen between the ears of a galloping horse.'

In 1929 LE's very attractive book, *Huntsmen Past and Present*, was published. He dedicated it to 'the Masters and hunt servants of the many packs with whom I have had happy days, but to the latter in particular in grateful recognition of the fact that their skill and devotion to their duties are in no way explained by any wages they receive'.

In 1929, too, Ethel and he went to Gibraltar where they stayed at the Convent (Government House), their hosts being the Governor and Commander-in-Chief and his wife. General Sir Alexander Godley (a former Master of the Staff College Draghounds and member of the Irish Guards polo team) and LE had much in common. He wanted the now celebrated sporting artist to paint some pictures of that most extraordinary institute of the old British Colonial days, the Royal Calpé hunt. LE, with his excellent sense of what has been, of history, promptly delved into the origin of the Royal Calpé and came up with the following hypothesis. It probably originated with the Duke of Wellington's pack in the Peninsular, whose huntsman, Tom Crane was briefly captured, complete with his hounds. Be that as it may LE's introduction to the Gibraltar hunt gave him the notion of a picture of Crane being rounded up by Napoleon's dragoons for inclusion in his book, *Sport in War*.

[80]

The Wilton on Gallows Hill (Watercolour and gouache on grey paper)

The Berkeley near Rockhampton (Watercolour)

Lord Hugh Percy's Beagles (Watercolour)

The Scarteen Black-and-Tans (Watercolour)

If there is a connection between Wellington's hounds and the Royal Calpé it is the same pack that the First Guards kennelled at Cadiz in 1812, for those were adopted by the 29th Regiment in 1814 and taken to the Rock. The Calpé became 'Royal' in 1906, the hunt buttons bearing the double crown of Edward VII and Alfonso XIII. LE's research showed that the 8th Duke of Beaufort brought 20 couple of the Badminton hounds to Gib in 1861 and that 'excellent sport was shown' with the combined packs.

'To a stay-at-home like myself,' said Edwards, 'it was a strange experience going fox-hunting on foreign soil, to ride out past the British sentries at Gib and then through the heavily guarded customs barrier at La Linea, through the Guardia Civil and numerous other uniformed (smaller) fry, all of whom were polite and pleasant, but quite obviously considered us mad. In fact, the *mise en scène* was quite different from an English hunting morning, with donkeys carrying large burdens, which concealed a mass of saddle sores, and, as contrast, the fat well-turned-out mules of the Spanish Army. The passing hunt aroused no interest or curiosity, the Spaniard carried on with whatever he happened to be doing (usually nothing) without looking up. . . .

'A hunt in the open country was very picturesque as at that time of year the

[81]

landscape was a sea of golden bloom, with the real sea and the "Rock" in the distance. I was singularly unsuccessful in trying to depict it! I might add a run through the cork woods was most interesting, with its sunlit glades and tiny farms, and its hidden railway with no fence, which we seemed to be continually crossing. In fact, it was all full of the unexpected, especially in the Soto Gordo which was full of "riot", deer (both red and roe), wild pig, semi-wild pig and tame pig of inextricably mixed descent, since the impecunious Spaniard ties his sows up on the edge of the forest hoping a passing wild boar will be smitten with the ladies' charms. Occasionally one met a bull in the glades, either remotely or nearly related to the fighting animals. . . . The Calpé Point-to-Point was held whilst I was there and the Spanish farmers turned out in force for the free lunch. I thought English farmers fair trenchermen, but I simply could not compete with the local number of courses.'

One of his oil studies, conjuring the customary Edwards local atmosphere and veracity, adorns the jacket of Gordon Fergusson's *Hounds are Home (the History of the Royal Calpé Hunt)*. Among other charming compositions which he painted while staying with the Godleys – all full of Andalusian *ambiente* – were *The Royal Calpé Hounds Above Guardacorte*, *The Earthstopper*, *The Royal Calpé Hunt Point-to-Point Meeting* and *Meet at The Duke of Kent's Farm*.

Disappointed follower of the Royal Calpé. The Barrier, Gibraltar, 1929

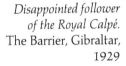

[82]

IV

HARK FORRARD
AND HARK BACK

THE HORSEMAN

My song is of the Horseman — who woke the world's unrest,
To slake a king's ambition or serve a maid's behest;
Who bore aloft the love-gage and reaped the rich reward;
Who swayed the purple banner and swung the golden sword!

My song is of the Horseman! steel wrist and iron thigh,
In whatsoever saddle, beneath whatever sky!
Who breaks the road for Empire; who leads the hope forlorn;
Who rides with whip and knee-pad; who rides with rope and horn!

My song is of the Horseman who leads us through the vale,
Who dares the deepest river and risks the stoutest rail!
Who, 'neath the roaring race-stand, rides down to fence or fall;
Who bends above the boar-spear; who drives the dancing ball!

My song is of the Horseman, the centaur of all time
Who stole for us the freedom of colts of every clime!
Who wore the spurs of mastery, who held the reins of pride,
Who left the world a heritage of sons to rule and ride!

[83]

Up! Swear by bit and saddle-cloth, by crupper, cinch, and horn,
The spurs our grandsires buckled by our sons' sons shall be worn!
Let oil, nor steam, nor wings of dream deprive us of our own —
The wide world for a kingdom and the saddle for a throne!

Will H. Ogilvie

(From *Sketches in Stable*
and Kennel)

The Moroccan coast had been the resort of several English artists towards the end of the 19th century and in the early years of the 20th, among them G. D. Armour and that considerable master of animal form, Joseph Crawhall, (who won the Tangier Hunt Cup three times). LE, too, found himself attracted to that exotic strand and its sporting hinterland. From Gibraltar the Edwardses took the ferry to Tangier, where they stayed with Admiral Sir Guy Gaunt in time to participate in the club's annual pig-sticking meet, which took place some twelve miles south of the town. Having been provided with horses and spears they drew a place in a narrow ravine, an obvious spot, LE forecast, for the boar to break.

So it proved: 'Suddenly I see what looks like a black carpet bag being rolled end over end down the hillside opposite — it is a pig! Unfortunately, at this moment my neighbour's bay stallion becomes bored with inaction and emits a series of shrill and piercing neighs. Will this turn our pig? Apparently not, for he merely swings a trifle more to the right, and off we go to try to intercept him. We clatter over rocks, crash through bushes, jump thorns, and at intervals get glimpses of Mr Piggy as he makes for the cliff above us. Several horsemen of another "beat" have joined in and try to cut him off by getting above him; but the Admiral on the aforementioned

Pigsticking, Tangier, 1929. 'He merely swings a trifle more to the left and off we go to intercept him'

[85]

talkative horse sticks to him until the pig "props" suddenly, spins round and delivers an upward cut as the horse passes over him. Nevertheless, first spear is given *en passant*, and as he swings round he is stuck again in the shoulder and held, the horse most gallantly not giving ground an inch as the pig struggles in dumb rage to get to closer quarters. Several more spears come up, but not one horse will close in, so the stout man of the party, in both senses of the word, jumps off and delivers the *coup de grâce* on foot. Not a big pig in avoirdupois, but big enough in heart, for he never attempted to avoid a "scrap" with superior numbers.'

The inveterate field sportsman goes on further to describe the excitement, colour and smell of Moroccan pig-sticking and to add many sketches to his portfolio before returning to Gibraltar and the Convent whence he travels to the *corridas*. That was just before the Primo de Rivera government decreed — not for the sake of the nags, but to appease the sensitivities of tourists — that picadors' horses should be padded against the horns and the deadly weight behind them, and LE was duly appalled at the 'ghastly injuries'. As for the spectacle of bullfighting in general he shows a little less compassion: 'It is definitely not a sport to our notions, for the bull, however gallantly he fights, is doomed in advance. Nonetheless we need waste no sympathy on him; like the gamecock he is bred to fight, and could he state his case would doubtless prefer the bull-ring to the slaughter-house.'

LE's cogent feel for 'what has been' was focused more on the history of the Romans, the people of the Stuart period, the story of Scotland and the great coaching days than any other eras. But he was ready to portray pretty well any sporting event at any time, as he shows through the pages of Lionel Dawson's *Sport in War*, in which he takes us to the theatre of Marlborough's wars, to Regency India, to the British Army in the Peninsular, to watch a steeplechase during the Crimean campaign — with that intrepid adventuress, Mrs Duberly — to the Western front and the Salonika of the First World War, and to India's Peshawar Vale jackal hunt in the 1920s. He pored over the remnants of the old Roman road that loses and finds itself again at Buckholt; he often returned, in his imagination, to the days of his Gamul ancestors; while the past of the Highland moors and their glens and villages always fascinated him.

In 1932 he and his great friend and brother brush, Frank Wallace — a man with an exceptionally sound knowledge of the Highlands and their traditions — went on a motor tour, making sketches and collecting material for their joint production, *A Stuart Sketch Book.* Most of that was done from Wallace's 18th century house, Old

Corriemony in Glen Urquhart, north Inverness-shire. 'Frank . . . was well able "to kindle a spark in ashes long grown cold" so it was less difficult than I expected to re-people the deserted glens and long empty battlefields,' LE tells us, and goes on to describe the problems of ensuring accuracy *à propos* the details of the '45, in particular the battles of Falkirk and Culloden. 'There is something very fascinating in attempting to visualise and reconstruct a long-forgotten battle scene, and how easy it is to make a hash of it. One can read up the period and study the uniforms, contemporary drill books and so forth and still go wrong. . . .' Yet, owing to the great pains he took in securing the authentic detail, he rarely made a serious mistake.

Wallace and he combined, too, in *Hunting and Stalking the Deer*, a most erudite – as well as a lavishly illustrated – tome in which Edwards contributes the hunting and Exmoor knowledge and Wallace the stalking and most of the naturalist material. The book includes essays on red, roe and fallow deer, measurements of record stag heads, abnormalities and accidents, 'leaves from a stalker's notebook', buck-hunting and hind-hunting, deer coursing, harbouring, poaching and even one magnificently successful combined painting. Edwards and Wallace have been acclaimed by many authorities as the two best painters of deer of this century (Balfour Browne not excepted). LE's skill in featuring the might and majesty of the Highland deserts has won unqualified admiration from many who have been born and bred there.

[87]

Goodnight to Skye

Above Glen Urquhart

[88]

Deer crossing a stream   *Frank Wallace*

He worked much in watercolour, a medium demanding spontaneous execution
from rough notes and memory, with little or no time for second thoughts, modification
or correction. But it was a medium in which swiftly-accurate, quick-working Edwards
excelled. By now he had long been a member of the Royal Institute of Painters in
Water Colours and no man deserved the letters RI after his name more than he did.

Following the Highlands, the racecourses, Exmoor, polo grounds, gymkhanas and
horse show arenas, winters found him back on his beloved hunting circuit in Britain
and Ireland — his own chauffeur, Rogers, was at the wheel now — painting scenes
in specific landscape settings, presentation and commemorative pictures and storing
up the wonderful fund of stories which he recorded so eloquently for posterity. The
Master of the Taunton Vale Harriers told him that, when, in 1918, he offered his
huntsman, Rickards, a cheque 'to square up outstanding debts during my absence',
the good man replied 'Not at all, sir, I'll give you a cheque for the money I've saved

[89]

Back chat!

during the war!' LE recalls Will Dale, huntsman to the Duke of Beaufort, drawing an osier bed on foot and getting stuck in the mud. When a fox was holloaed away the old huntsman jumped on his horse leaving his boots behind and, to the delight of the field, finished the run in his socks. He remembers an 'irascible MFH of the old school' cursing a hard-riding stranger and ending with 'I suppose, sir, you think because it is a fine day there must be a fine scent!' And another addressing a group of women 'chattering like magpies' at the covertside with the words: 'Will you please be quiet! I can't listen to two bitch packs giving tongue at the same time!' He over-heard an amateur huntsman, upon whose heels a certain equestrienne was forever riding and jumping, shout out in sheer desperation, 'Will whoever owns this woman kindly take her home!' One day in Hampshire he recalls a professional addressing a hurdle maker: 'Your mate tells me you've seen a fox; about what time would that be?' 'Well I don't remember exactly' came the rejoinder, 'but it would be 'bout dinner time Monday!'

LE's *Country Life* articles are full of venatic wisdom. In the issue of November 13, 1938, he describes the breeding of the Pentyrch and the country they have to

[90]

negotiate, incorporating answers to various questions he posed to the Master and discussing with intense interest the characteristics of the hounds. 'It is very noticeable that the modern Welsh hound is far more like the hound depicted by the famous sporting artists of the past than he is to the fashionable foxhound of to-day – or should we say yesterday? For the type is changing again, judging by what one has seen on the flags in recent years. . . . The rough-coated variety of Welsh hounds of Glamorganshire are far from being all white or all rough-coated and litters throw back away from their parents to lemon and white; rough will throw smooth white, and smooth black-and-tan. For certain of the old Welsh breeds are black-and-tan or grizzled tan, and have wiry rather than really rough coats. But when all is said, there are really remarkably few packs of pure-bred Welsh in existence. . . .'

He loved to see his paintings and drawings and the little essays he wrote about them published between the covers of books of which many more, such as *My Scottish Sketch Book, The Fox, Sketches in Stable and Kennel, Thy Servant the Horse, A Sportsman's Bag, Beasts of the Chase* and *The Passing Seasons* followed. In 1938 he composed the illustrations for R. C. Lyle's *The Aga Khan's Horses*, in which such names as Bahram,

[91]

*The 1936 Derby winner:
Mahmoud.* 'He drew
them exactly as he saw
them, which was not
always in a very
flattering pose or
condition'

Friar's Daughter, Mumtaz Mahal, Teresina, Dastur and Mahmoud recall some of the great events of the Turf during the 1930s. Each time one of those champions was paraded before him, he drew him exactly as he saw him, which was not always in a very flattering pose or condition. His rendering of Golden Miller, aged 23, in 1950 was regarded by the pundits as 'one of the cleverest of all equine portraits'. But although racing events, whether on the flat or over the sticks, occupied much of his artistic time between the wars and he achieved the most brilliant impressions

*Portrait of
Denis Aldridge*

of speed and colour and animal and human athleticism, the racecourse – as he told the Aldridges and others – was far from being his favourite scene.

Edwards was over 60 by the time Hitler's war began. While he and Ethel continued to live contentedly enough at Buckholt, he raised and commanded a mounted troop of the Home Guard. Derrick, Lindsay and Ken were all away in the Army, but Marjorie was able to remain in her profession as a teacher. Just as LE's creative lifestyle was abruptly curtailed in 1914, so it was more or less cut off in 1939.

Apart from his contributions of articles and pictures to *Country Life*, his artistic work slowed down to a trickle. It was a time for reflection. He had lost both his surviving brothers in the 1920s. Arthur, the manager of a Welsh slate quarry – and devoted fly-fisherman – died in 1922, and Fitz, who retired from the Army in 1919, died ten years later. Between the wars Lionel and Ethel lost many more of their friends. It was a time for LE the patriot and farmer and sportsman to look back on the golden days.

[93]

The Aldridges at the
Atherstone Hunt Ball, 1935

LE in the mid-1930s

His *Scarlet and Corduroy* was published in 1941 and dedicated to Arthur – 'To the Memory of A.G.E. an Impecunious Gentleman, who loved both Salmon-Fishing and helping Lame Dogs over Stiles, both Expensive Pursuits'. Its preface is headed with Schopenhauer – 'Today comes only once and never returns' – while its chapters are full of hunting and fishing memories, comparisons of the many different hunters he has ridden and censure and appraisal of modern farming methods. They are larded, too, with nostalgia for the days of childhood and youth.

He repines the passing of both horse and oxen ploughing; and he complains of the raw deal given by the Government to farmers, until the exigencies of war prove their real worth and importance; of artificial fertilisers; of the removal of hedgerows in favour of barbed wire; and of the pollution of rivers – which leads him on to compare brother Arthur's predilection with his own. 'However, river pollution is not a major problem for me, for I am no fisherman in the sense my brother was. He had for it an enthusiasm which only fox-hunting raises in me. We had the same love of the riverside, although he had no patience with my views. He looked on me as one who keeps an eye on the water and one on the heavens, and he held,

[94]

Arthur Edwards and
trout rod on the Dart

with the Scriptures, that "To everything there is a season and a time for every purpose under heaven" maintaining that you go out fishing to fish. If I quoted Izaac Walton:

> *So I the fields and meadows green may view,*
> *And daily by fresh water walk at will,*

and "taking therein no little delectation" as the aforesaid Izaac says, he would reply with this little tale: "I had a certain buttonhole acquaintance who used, like myself,

to hunt on shanks's mare. He always had a copy of *The Times* in his pocket, and used to sit on a gate to read it whilst hounds were drawing cover, or at a check. He presumably had some half-hearted love of hunting or he would not have been there, but I maintain his is a parallel case to the fisherman who shares his love of beauty with his love of fishing – in other words, his is no very ardent love".'

LE shakes his head at the changing face of the social hierarchy on the land and thus the attitudes of society. 'It is a curious weakness of all classes of the community in these so-called democratic days to try to appear to be better off than their neighbours. . . . Unfortunately the relation between master and man on the farm is not quite on the friendly footing it once was . . . whilst no one can dispute the desirability of National Health, Pensions, Unemployment Insurance and so forth, yet they have somehow taken away the mutual responsibility from master to man and vice versa. Consequently, there is no particular incentive to consult each others' interests. The employee merely becomes hired labour and the master the man who pays it. . . .'

He regrets the coming of the combustion engine, looks back with unqualified

Sandown, 1948
(Watercolour on grey
paper)

*The Hon. Dorothy
Paget's Straight Deal, by
Solario*, 1949 (Canvas)

Cheltenham, 1950
(Watercolour)

The Meet at Crick — the
Pytchley, 1952
(Canvas)

admiration at the great coaching era. In a memoir in a 1941 *Country Life* he remembers
an old Cockney groom and coachman called Dick whom he first knew in the
glamorous late Victorian era and then again among the motor cars of the 1930s.
'It was a smart London in those days,' he says of Dick's life in the 1890s. 'Now
chauffeurs lounging in their seats outside the big shops make a poor display in comparison with the liveried coachmen, grooms and footmen they have displaced. The
courtyard of Burlington House on the day of the Academy private view was a marvellous sight in the 'nineties. The crowd of servants with their top-hats, stand-up collars,
white gloves and dark-coloured liveries of the comparatively impecunious, and the
cocked hats, gold lace, white breeches, white stockings, and buckled shoes of the
Royalties or aristocracy were in themselves a spectacle. . . .

'Some years passed before I saw Dick again, and then, as I was looking at some
cars in the local car mart, I saw an old man with pursed lips hissing away to himself
as he polished a car. The face seemed vaguely familiar. I went in and spoke to him.
It was Dick. "Well, you appear to have got a soft job this time, Dick," I said. "Oh,

yuss, It's not too bad and pay's fairly good, but I 'ates the job. In fact it fair gives me the creeps to come in 'ere of a mornin' and see these damned tin boxes standin' exactly as they was night afore and silent as the blinkin' grave. I misses the stampin' 'ooves and the cheerful whicker of 'osses waitin' for their breakfast".'

So far as 'osses were concerned Dick was clearly a man after the artist's heart, and, as for Britain, the nation of LE's youth was infinitely preferable to that of the autumn of his life.

It is difficult to think of an autobiography that tells you less about its author than the brief *Reminiscences of a Sporting Artist*, (most of which had already featured, chapter by chapter, in *Country Life*). But the book – written towards the end of the Second World War – does contain a fine essay on animal art, while in another chapter, entitled *Ars Longa Vita Brevis*, he drops some gems of wisdom for aspiring animal and sporting artists to take up and digest. He begins with a broad brush. 'The delineator of animal life has never been taken very seriously by either artist or critic, yet he belongs to a peculiarly British school of painting, . . . Most of the early painters made a poor fist of animals in their pictures. Yet the Greeks in sculpture showed the horse with remarkable exactitude of observation. Velasquez and Vandyck were the first great

horse painters. To modern eyes their horses seem unconvincing, though it is not the artists who are wrong, but the modern spectator. . . .' And he reserves special praise for Meissonier and Aimé Morot ('his *Rezonville — Charge* is probably still the finest example of horses in violent action by any artist').

For the beginner he recommends '. . . two lines of approach. Supposing he were to take the ordinary curriculum of any art school he would be turned out with a certain technical knowledge which would be of immense help. It would have given him facility and speed of execution very necessary to anyone attempting to portray animals who in natural conditions never remain in one position long. On the other hand the enthusiast with no knowledge of technique, whose love of animals is such that he is compelled to attempt to put on paper what he sees, may perhaps in the end become the better animal painter. He will have obtained the really essential knowledge from nature at first hand, and not from imitating the methods of other artists.'

He has a lot more to say about effecting the illusion of speed, and then goes on to warn against the pitfalls of inaccuracy in hunting dress, saddlery, horses, hounds ('the commonest error is to make them running with their mouths shut'), foxes, cattle

[99]

and sheep. 'With regard to mounted sports' (other than hunting), he thinks 'the student should have little difficulty in finding sufficient material from the daily press, and as for racing and polo, they are sports than can be witnessed by anyone within easy reach of London, but the latter game is full of traps for the artist'. He warns that 'no animals so utterly defeat the artist as the deer tribe', omitting to add that they never really even began to defeat him!

By the time *Reminiscences* was published (1947) sporting England had returned to nearly all its old activity and colour; and, as though to proclaim that the nation put austerity behind her, that November the Household Cavalry wore full dress for the first time since 1939 – for the wedding of HRH Princess Elizabeth and Lieutenant Philip Mountbatten RN. Race meetings, horse shows and polo tournaments began to re-emerge with all their pre-war panoply, and the Hursley hounds – on the hunt committee of which Edwards would serve for 43 years – met with their Masters, hunt servants and leading subscribers in scarlet. Picking up the threads where he dropped them in 1939, he was on his artist's circuit to other hunt countries again, too, and the 1950s and '60s beckoned, and would not deceive him.

(From *Hunting the Fox*)

V

THE FINISH

THE VETERAN

He asks no favour from the Field, no forward place demands,
Save what he claims by fearless heart and light and dainty hands;
No man need make a way for him at ditch or gap or gate,
He rides on level terms with all, if not at equal weight.

His eyes are somewhat dimmer than they were in days of yore,
A blind fence now might trap him where it never trapped before;
But when the rails stand clean and high, the walls stand big and bare,
There's no man rides so boldly as there's no man rides so fair.

There is no other in the Field so truly loved as he;
We better like to see him out than any younger three;
And yet one horseman day by day rides jealous at his rein —
Old Time that smarts beneath the whip of fifty years' disdain.

He crowds him at his fences, for he envies his renown;
Some day he'll cross him at a leap and bring a good man down,
And Time will take a long revenge for years of laughing scorn,
And fold the faded scarlet that was ne'er more nobly worn.

[101]

Here's luck! Oh! good, grey sportsman! May Time be long defied
By careful seat and cunning hand and health and heart to ride,
And when that direful day be come that surely shall befall,
We'll know you still unbeaten, save by Time that beats us all!

Will H. Ogilvie

(From *Hunting the Fox*)

'At various times,' said LE, 'one gets glimpses of the early efforts of some of our famous artists, but it is my impression that none of them in their youthful efforts showed any marked superiority over the average child of similar age. Several, I am told, showed no great talent even in their later student days, and were advised by their art masters to seek other professions as they would never make a living out of art! This was a rash statement as the work of even advanced art students is usually little guide to their future. Brilliant students, winners of scholarships, and so forth, of my acquaintance, never did anything afterwards, whilst others, that neither masters nor students thought anything remarkable, turned out well. It is no fault of the art masters, and it always annoys me when I see how little credit some of the top-sawyers in the art world give to their teachers. Their attitude appears to be "Alone I did it"!

'It is sometimes held up against art masters that their own work is often pretty moderate. That may be sometimes true, but if many teachers cannot draw, many good artists cannot teach! Teaching is an art in itself, and in really good teachers it is a gift which has been developed by both training and practice.

'I am inclined to think that, with a few brilliant exceptions, artists develop late in comparison with other professions. This explains why I think little value can be obtained from criticism of early work. . . .'

Those comments are particularly interesting in view of the following story. One of LE's warmest admirers before the war was a Downside schoolboy. Peter Biegel, whose over-riding ambition was to be a sporting artist, wrote to Edwards from Downside asking if he might be allowed to study under him for a while. The boy also enclosed a sketch. Would Mr Edwards criticise it? Would he send him a little sketch in return? LE complied with that. But no, he couldn't take Peter under his wing. If he agreed to all such requests he'd never get on with his own work. The war came, Biegel joined up, and, being badly wounded during the Normandy landings, was invalided. He then resumed his drawing and painting with fresh eye and fresh vigour.

One day in 1947 Biegel travelled with his portfolio by rail from Salisbury to London, hoping to sell some of his work for Christmas cards. Knowing there would be no restaurant car he took a packet of sandwiches with him. When the elderly gentleman who shared his compartment returned from an abortive expedition down the corridor — venting his rage at Great Western for not putting on their programmed restaurant car — Biegel offered him a share of his sandwiches. The elderly gentleman

Edwards's pupil, Peter Biegel, at work in the United States during his later career. 'That was how another very successful delineator of horse and hound came to blossom'

eagerly accepted. They started chatting and it soon transpired that Biegel's travelling companion was none other than Lionel Edwards. With some trepidation the tyro opened his portfolio and showed the maestro his paintings. LE was impressed. Would Peter Biegel like to come to Buckholt for a period of study? Indeed he would!

Biegel says that 'The maestro disclaimed any genius, but thought he might have a tip or two to offer . . . he was a hard task master . . . the Buckholt studio was light and airy, but Lionel Edwards didn't believe in living in a hothouse; most of his work was done outdoors, sometimes in the freezing cold. . . .' Anyhow, that was how another very successful delineator of horse and hound came to blossom. Nor did LE fail to teach Peter Biegel how to achieve the effect of mud and rain. Biegel's wonderful facility for translating the movement of horse and hound into pencil-stroke and paint, thus acquired, has been warmly and rightly praised.

Years later Biegel was shown another facet of LE's modesty. While Edwards was

Mrs H. G. Gregson, MFH. 'Lionel took infinite pains to get the colours, markings and conformation of my hounds correct' she said. 'The result was he turned each into the individual it was'

staying in West Sussex with Mrs H. G. Gregson, the celebrated Master (1939–1960) of the Crawley and Horsham, Biegel, working on a nearby commission, drove over to visit them. Mrs Gregson brought out a portrait of a terrier by Geoffrey Sparrow. 'Just take a look at that, Peter!' said LE. 'Isn't it wonderful? Now that's something neither you nor I could ever achieve.'

'Lionel stayed with me three or four times,' Mollie Gregson recalls. 'The chief impression I had was that he combined being absolutely natural, quite unaffected, with delightful courtesy and a marvellous sense of humour. . . . For the portrait of my huntsman, Denton, on the Downs, my chauffeur drove us up to Chanctonbury. Lionel made some quick but careful sketches there, then he asked to be taken to the kennels and stables, where he drew individual portraits of each hound and horse to be included in the picture. He took infinite pains to get the colours, markings and conformation correct. The result was he turned each into the individual it was.'

[105]

Charles Chafer, MFH. In his judgement 'Lionel's eye for detail and his gift for achieving animal likenesses were quite remarkable'

Charles Chafer, a Yorkshireman, who was Master of the Derwent and with whom LE stayed both before and after the war, echoes that verdict. 'Lionel's eye for detail and his gift for achieving animal likenesses were quite remarkable. When he went to the kennels to make sketches of our hounds, he drew them precisely as he saw them – the same shapes, colours, attitudes and positions, so that each was instantly recognisable – whereas, for rough sketches, any other artist I've seen working merely drew the outlines of something that looked like foxhounds. . . . I prize the sketches he did of my favourite hounds as much as anything.'

Mr Chafer's memoir, which I have on tape, continues like this. 'Undoubtedly Lionel's first love was hunting, of which he was very knowledgeable. He loved painting, but he loved hunting even more. While he enjoyed the ride, he rode essentially for the sake of hunting. Houndwork fascinated him, hence the pack of bloodhounds he once kept. Whenever he came to stay with us he always knew where hounds were meeting. He would go out early in the morning and say, "I don't think the light's going to be good enough today to paint, Charles, so let's go hunting." He possessed an astounding memory for detail. He once painted a presentation picture for me of a farmer called Neville Danby who hunted the Derwent hounds throughout the war. One evening two years later Lionel rang me and said he'd just remembered making a mistake in the painting – had anyone noticed it? I told him, "Certainly not, so

[106]

My dear Charles,
   The mare arrived yesterday rather late (10 pm). The driver would not admit he had lost the way, but obviously he had! They never gave me their names or address, so I don't know what I owe (you or them?).

   The head collar sent was broken, no matter, but I forgot to ask you for my martingale – and Andrews says we have no other – also if you have a spare surcingle I could do with it – I believe I sent one with her, mine is too small for her fat tummy.

   The few fine days have vanished – wind and rain, most annoying. I had just started a picture of Bathurst and the background was Cirencester House with the virginia creeper – turned red – now it's all come down!

   Rather curious coincidence – I've got commissions to paint the MFH's of both V.W.H. packs.

   I painted the joint-Masters of the Four Burrow recently and went cubbing several times, chiefly on my feet. It was interesting to see that even that was no great hindrance. It was on the banks thus – and did not stop anyone!

   All the same I must stop!
   Yours ever, Lionel.

far as I know." He said, "Well, I remember now, Danby's left-handed, and I painted him carrying the horn in his right hand. I suppose it will have to be artistic licence" . . .'

LE's friend Captain Jack Gilbey, who prized the largest collection of the artist's work, enjoyed the privilege of choosing the background for his picture of the Essex hounds and of watching LE paint the scene, in front of White Roding. This is how he describes the experience in *Country Life*:

'With his usual thoroughness Lionel went out for a day with the hunt in order to take stock of the huntsman, his horse and the pack. In the meantime he had asked me to suggest a typical Essex setting, and I thought I could not do better than choose the distant view of the village of White Roding, with undulating ploughland in foreground and middle distance, which had been familiar to me from boyhood.

'On the day I watched him at work I was very glad of my warm overcoat and scarf, as the Rodings in March can be a very cold spot, especially when one is on the wrong side of the hedge and facing an east wind. I observed that the easel which he had set up swayed considerably, and the drawing-board required the usual piece of string with a weight attached to it to keep it steady. All the time that he was getting things ready I noticed he was constantly looking at his subject. From a somewhat untidy paintbox he drew a line across the drawing-board. This important line set the limit of the foreground. A second line fixed the extent and depth of the land-

Captain Jack Gilbey. 'He prized the largest collection of the artist's work'

scape in the middle distance, and then, starting from the left, he lightly dotted in the salient features, such as the road, trees and cottages.

'What interested me particularly, apart from the quickness and sureness with which all this was accomplished, was the space that he allotted to the foreground, the middle distance and the sky – the last named it seemed, monopolised considerably more than two-thirds of the drawing-board. As he worked he smoked incessantly. It was not until seven years later that he gave up smoking for the sake of his health.

'"Let's have a go now at this Essex sky," he suddenly exclaimed. And I remember looking at a cold, grey and featureless sky and wondering how he would transpose this on to his drawing-board. But, like the other details, it apparently presented no difficulties.

'And so the morning wore on; it was now 12.30 p.m., and he had been working for $2\frac{1}{2}$ hours. We motored home for lunch and were back on the scene once more at 2.30 p.m. The second session lasted until 4 o'clock.

'Conditions were slightly better in the afternoon, and for nearly half an hour the

[108]

sun made a valiant attempt to warm us, at the same time lighting up the distant scene and bringing into sharp relief the windmill, the church – even the tombstones – and the cottage buildings, a situation which the artist was quick to take advantage of.

'Before we left, he had written in pencil some notes on the top of the picture and signed and dated it in the left-hand corner. The sketch was complete.

'The following month, April, the second water-colour drawing accompanying this article was also completed. But whereas the former was entirely an out-of-doors study, the latter was executed in the artist's studio at home.

'When later I saw this larger picture, which measured 30 ins by 20 ins, in the studio, Mr Edwards smilingly remarked, "I have given you an extremely well-behaved field. Every member of the hunt is depicted on the left of the road and only the huntsman is with his hounds."

'I was pleased that he had done this, as much more of the landscape was thus made visible! This sketch of White Roding, with its cold grey sky, its wide expanse

Out with the Hursley
on his 80th birthday

The model is
Col. Sir John Miller,
the Crown Equerry

of gently undulating fields of brown plough, its trees that stand out peculiarly black against the sky-line, gives a faithful reproduction of a typical part of Essex hunting country. . . .'

LE could also appreciate that art form in which no artist's licence is possible – the art of the photographer. Between the 1930s and 1960s he was admiring the work of Frank Meads, (a pre-war *Country Life* staff photographer). Meads, who specialised in hunting photography, generally contrived to produce the equivalent of 'a Lionel Edwards sky' in his prints. LE was so impressed that he painted a picture of Frank and his son Jim (very well known in the world of venery today) photographing a hunt, and another of Jim on his own in the same act. LE also sketched the frontispiece for Frank Meads's collection, *They Meet at Eleven*.

While Peter Biegel was the only full-time pupil the old master took on, he continued to give Denis Aldridge an incidental lesson whenever he stayed with him during Aldridge's secretaryship of the Quorn (1947–58) and afterwards when the Aldridges moved to Wymondham. They always encouraged him to use their home as a base for his many commissions in the Shires.

'Lionel was a most accomplished horseman', said Mrs Aldridge, 'and whatever horse he rode went well for him. In all the years Denis knew him he remembers

[111]

With friends at Buckholt

With Denis Aldridge at Wymondham. Edwards entitled this snapshot 'the empty decanter'

only one occasion when he had a fall. Hounds had just gone away, and the large field, pushing and shoving to get with them, came to a very big fence with a gate further up the field. Lionel decided to jump the fence rather than await his turn at the gate. As he approached it, his horse at the last minute suddenly decided that *he* preferred the gate, and they quickly parted company. Lionel did a most amusing sketch of this episode for his *Leicestershire Sketch Book.*

'With his great knowledge of hunting,' Mrs Aldridge continues, 'Lionel was meticulous over every detail of horse and rider and got people's seats to perfection, so that, seeing one of his paintings across a room, one knew instantly who the figures were meant to be. He enjoyed depicting well turned-out men and women (though he did not give such minute attention to his own appearance, rather following Jorrocks' adage, "I goes out to please myself, and not to astonish others!").

'In February, 1958, Lionel stayed with us for the Melton Hunt Club cross-country Race, an event which had been revived after about a hundred years and aroused enormous interest among all hunting people. This was the first occasion of the revival. No one who was there could ever forget that day. We woke to heavy grey skies and at about eight o'clock, sleet began to fall which soon turned to snow. It was bitterly cold. Denis went off early to collect his horse, Rocket, and rode on to Upper Broughton in a blinding snowstorm.

'Lionel and I followed later and arrived to find a surprising number of competitors,

C. Denton with the Crawley and Horsham Hounds at Chanctonbury, 1960 (Watercolour)

The Royal Calpé at Duke of Kent's Farm (Watercolour and gouache on grey paper)

*Inspection of the
Household Cavalry
Mounted Regiment,
Hyde Park, 1959*

*Presentation of New
Standards to the
Household Cavalry by
HM the Queen, 1963*

Lionel and Ethel in the 1960s

horse boxes, trailers and cars, seemingly from all over England, and some roads already blocked. We got out of the car to find visibility down to about a field, and the balloons tethered as guide marks indiscernible in the gloom. The snowstorm then turned into a horizontal blizzard and we could really see nothing. Lionel, having gone with the object of painting the race, was not going to be deterred by the elements, and announced that he would get out to have a look, and would be just down the road. He vanished into the blizzard and I waited. After a while I began to get rather uneasy. I had caught sight of the race through the blizzard so knew it must be over, and still there was no sign of Lionel. I had visions of him having fallen into a snowdrift or lying covered by snow in a ditch. I began to drive about asking everyone if they had seen him, but no one had. I even tried to penetrate a solid mass of loudly-celebrating people in the pub; my anxious voice was lost in the hubbub.

'Eventually I made my miserable way home convinced of a disaster. But there was Lionel, sitting by the fire, cosily chatting to a friend who had given him a lift, not being able to find me. He had been soaked to the skin, and his precious sketch book reduced to pulp, but in spite of everything he had made a sketch which de-veloped later into a superb picture of the race. . . .

[113]

'One incident which always made Lionel laugh occurred when he was staying with us. An American mutual friend was very anxious to be painted with his wife at the Quorn opening meet at Kirby Gate. All was arranged and we were just starting out when a message came that our friend had decided at the last minute to hunt with the Belvoir. His wife was going to follow in the car, but they still wanted to be painted as if at Kirby Gate.

'We drove with all possible speed to Kirby Gate where Lionel sketched the background, and then set off to find the Belvoir hounds at the other end of the country. We eventually caught up with the subject, but his wife had to be dug out of the depths of a car to sit on someone's horse. I afterwards heard they were delighted with the result of this rather unusual exercise. . . .'

One very important assignment in the Shires was a commemorative portrait of the Pytchley meeting at Crick in 1952 when Colonel John and Captain George Lowther and Major Peter Borwick were Masters and Stanley Barker carried the horn – a most formidable and illustrious regime. The idea was to reflect the Barraud brothers' *Meet at Crick* painted in 1848 when Lord Alford had just relieved George Payne of the Mastership. LE's rendering was generally acclaimed as another sure triumph.

A much more complicated group was required of him in 1959. Lieutenant-Colonel Max Gordon, who was then nearing the end of his command of the Household Cavalry Mounted Regiment, wanted to give a picture of the annual inspection of the regiment mounted in Hyde Park – by the Major-General commanding the Household Brigade – as a leaving present. This was one of the artist's most difficult undertakings, and, being the perfectionist he was, LE was anxious that not a single detail of the uniforms or horse furniture should be incorrect. Having laid on a photographer to take shots of the first rehearsal from various angles, as *aide-memoires*, he proceeded to that parade in a staff car, escorted by an officer as adviser.

The officers who had taken part in the parade were astonished, on returning to their mess in Knightsbridge Barracks, to find him already sitting there holding a most comprehensive and attractive watercolour sketch of what he had in mind. But the remainder of the job was not so simple. For the actual ceremony he stood with sketch-pad and pencil among the public watching from the side of the field. Colonel Gordon then dispatched a trooper, complete with black horse and full dress, to Buckholt so that the artist would have a single model for authenticity. LE sent the commanding officer a series of sketch-cards with queries. Was this right for the trumpet-banner?

[114]

*Sketch for the
Presentation of
Standards to the
Household Cavalry*

Do the aigulettes of a corporal-of-horse hang like that? Is this correct for the headstall
of an officer's charger? And so on. Finally, quoting John Betjeman, he asked Colonel
Gordon whether he wanted the sky to be rather dour and monotonous, as it was
on the day — or 'a Lionel Edwards sky'? 'As it was' replied the Colonel. ('A decision
I've always since regretted,' he now tells me!)

It was four years later that LE was asked for a painting of the presentation of
new Standards to the Household Cavalry, an event that takes place every ten years
on Horse Guards parade, the presenter of those crimson silk and gilt-encrusted flags
being the Colonel-in-Chief of the Life Guards and the Blues, Her Majesty the Queen.
The Hyde Park study had been a good rehearsal for that. By the time he painted
the Horse Guards parade scene he was 85 years old. ('*Tempus* certainly does *fugit!*'
as he remarks.) What amazed everyone was that his hand was sufficiently steady
to render such minute detail unfalteringly, a task that would have daunted many
a 30-year-old limner.

Notwithstanding his unchallenged accomplishment LE could never be called an
'artist's artist'; he did not like London, let alone the environment of Chelsea studios;
he was not amused by the *beau monde*; he had little time for 'Art for Art's Sake'

or 'art with a capital A', and hardly any at all for *art nouveau* or the abstract. He was even rather aloof from his fellow animal-artists. He met Munnings (also born in 1878) on Exmoor and came away with the impression that 'he didn't seem to like me very much!'

Roy Heron, Cecil Aldin's biographer, wrote to me saying: 'Although Edwards and Aldin knew one another quite well, they were not really friends. They were different types. Edwards was lanky, calm and quiet, Aldin was short and extrovert. In the early days Aldin was rather annoyed that Edwards appeared to him to be following him around, painting the same hunts. But that was inevitable . . . Edwards sought atmosphere, Aldin the quick return from the sale of his prints, his art being his sole source of income. You probably know that, purely for sale purposes, Aldin provided keys to his hunting prints, making every member of the "field" identifiable. Edwards raised his eyes to the heavens at that! . . .' In short LE was as much an English country gentleman – with all the integrity and dignity, which (anyhow in his day) that implied – as he was an artist.

'During the last twenty years of his life,' Mrs Aldridge told me, 'Lionel painted

[116]

The Hon. Aylmer Tryon, founder of the Tryon Gallery. He was Edwards's exhibitor in the post-war years

entirely to give other people pleasure and for his own pleasure – certainly not for the money.' However that may be, naturally he wanted his work to be exhibited. A. E. Johnson, his faithful first agent, had long departed. He could not, in 1959 have chosen a worthier successor to exhibit him than the Hon. Aylmer Tryon, founder of the Tryon Gallery, to whom he was introduced by Frank Wallace and Jack Gilbey. After the war Aylmer Tryon set up his first animal and sporting gallery in Rowland Ward's premises in Piccadilly, and moved, independently, in 1959, to 41, Dover St. He was a gifted spotter of budding talent, and while the works of veterans like Thorburn, Wallace, Balfour-Browne, Harrison and Rickman hung on the Dover Street walls, those of his young protégés – Susan Crawford, David Shepherd, Timothy Greenwood, Peter Curling and others – followed with consummate success. The name Lionel Edwards was a golden addition to the gallery's list of artists and, had LE been born half a century or more later, Mr Tryon would probably have been the first dealer in sporting art to spot *his* budding talent! Aylmer Tryon lived (he still does) within easy driving distance of Buckholt, and often visited LE. 'He was tough and leathery as they come', he says; 'His studio was freezing. I insisted on a radiator when the

The studio as it was
when he was last at
work, 1966

His final picture: *The
Quorn changing horses
at Great Dalby.* 'A tired
hunter is being led
home'

[118]

temperature was below zero. Lionel laughed at that and always referred to the radiator as "the Aylmer"!'

LE did make one concession to the elements when he was in his 80s. He had a trailer attached to his car, from which to make his field sketches in winter, instead of standing in the snow and rain. But he was almost as prolific as he had been at 50. 33 out of 58 of the paintings at his 1961 Tryon exhibition were painted during the years 1956–58. And so it was at the next exhibition (1964), from which Jack Gilbey came away thinking: 'I see no reason why Lionel Edwards should not join the immortals such as the late G. E. Lodge, who was happily painting out of doors and in the winter months for several years after he had passed his 90th birthday.'

But Lodge was not riding to hounds in his 80s. In 1961 LE bought a new hunter, a mare called Grayling. When, after two or three seasons, she had to be put down, he followed the Hursley on foot or sat on his grandchildren's pony, watching from a vantage point. His eyesight was failing and the lustre sometimes went out of his colours; but in general, he kept in splendid health until the age of 88. Then, just as he was setting off from Buckholt to paint an equestrian portrait in Wales, he collapsed with a stroke and died peacefully in bed. The unfinished canvas on his studio easel was entitled *The Quorn Changing Horses at Great Dalby*. In the foreground of that painting a tired hunter is being led home. Thus departed Lionel Dalhousie Robertson Edwards, the finest hunting artist that ever lived. And ever will live, because, by and large, the old elegance of the hunting-field, along with the old beauty of the landscapes that Edwards knew, have vanished, never to return. We really only have his pictures – and those of no other artist – to know those times and that landscape by in their whole truth.

His had been an extraordinarily happy and fulfilled life.

'My own children', he had written, 'look on me as a diehard Tory.' And of course that was perfectly apt in the sense that he was a patriot and a lover of traditional values, one who believed in the virtues of clean play and due reward for hard work, freedom of the individual, personal independence and honest dealings. A whole generation has grown up and gone out into the world since he died. Doubtless there are many aspects of British life today that would sadden him; lax morals and manners, slovenliness and low standards of service, the lack of trust between classes, the defacing of the countryside, the impersonalisation of the farming business.

He would find, too, that the image of the hunting-field has changed for the worse; increased arable, widespread urbanisation, electrification of the railways, further reduction of hedgerows; and, in his beloved Ireland, the erosion of the banks, the proliferation of wire, both barbed and electric, and the prevalent trapping of foxes by pelt-traders. Also, everywhere in Britain, the comparative inelegance of those who hunt today; and the abandonment of hunting by many of its traditional families, whose place at the meets has frequently been taken by people who hunt only in order to ride and socialise.

The anti-hunting movement would perhaps grieve him as much as anything. For LE, the most compassionate of men and one who had made such a profound study of animal emotion, would surely have turned his back on the sport if it had been proved to be 'cruel', and not, as the case is, the salvation of a thousand other cruelties. LE took no delight in the killing of wild animals. 'It is not the quarry' – he would have concurred with Sir Walter Raleigh – 'but the chase that is the splendour of our days.'

On the other hand he would, if he returned today, find much that is good in the world of hunting, not the least of which is the well-supported enthusiasm for carefully planned hound-breeding and the remarkable adaptation of the foxhound to modern conditions, not to mention the determination of hunting's devotees, in the face of some violent opposition, that the sport shall thrive forever.

I am told that, if he had been given the choice, LE would have opted for death in the hunting-field. So let his old friend and creator-in-harness, Will Ogilvie, have the final word:

THE LAST FENCE

When the last fence looms up, I am ready
And I hope when the rails of it crack
There'll be nothing in front but the Master,
The huntsman, the fox, and the pack;
And I hope when fate bids me go under
In this last of my manifold spills,

That we're riding the line of a hill fox
With half a mile start to his hills.

I hope that last fence is a stiff one;
I hope, for the sake of our name,
They may say, 'If the task was beyond them
They both of them went at it game!'
And when the white girths flash above me,
And darkness comes down on the field,
Let them carry me home on a hurdle
As the Spartan went home on his shield.

And when I am out of the running
Let the good men go on with the pack;
I would not one comrade should falter,
I would not one friend should turn back;
And whether it be on the grass-land,
The hill-side, the heath or the loam,
Let the gallant ones keep going for'ard —
The slow ones can carry me home.

Let them bury me down in the churchyard,
But lay my good horse where he fell;
When the ditches are blind in the autumn
Some friend may remember and tell,

While under the thong of the west wind
The day-nettle trembles and stirs:
'Twas from here that a horseman undaunted
Went Home in his boots and his spurs.

[122]

BOOKS BY LIONEL EDWARDS

Beasts of the Chase. 1950

Famous Foxhunters. 1932

The Fox. 1949

Getting to Know your Pony. 1948

Horses and Ponies. A book of sketches. 1938

Horses and Riders. An anthology for horsemen (and horsewomen) of all ages. 1948

Hunting and Stalking the Deer (with H. Frank Wallace). 1927

Huntsmen Past and Present. 1929

A Leicestershire Sketch Book. 1935

The Lighter Side of Sport. 1940

My First Horse (with others). 1947

My Hunting Sketch Book. Vol. 1, 1928. Vol. 2, 1930

My Irish Sketch Book. 1929

My Scottish Sketch Book. 1929

Our Horses. 1945

The Passing Seasons. 1927

Reminiscences of a Sporting Artist. 1947

Scarlet and Corduroy. 1941

Seen from the Saddle. 1937

Sketches in Stable and Kennel (*De luxe* edition of 31 copies, containing a signed sketch by the author). 1933

Sketches in Stable and Kennel. Vol. 1, 1936. Vol. 2, 1953

A Sportsman's Bag (with an introduction by 'Crascredo'). 1937

A Sportsman's Sketch Book. 1953

Thy Servant the Horse. 1952

The Wiles of the Fox. 1932

BOOKS ILLUSTRATED BY LIONEL EDWARDS

Alderson, A. E. H.: *Pink and Scarlet, or Hunting as a School for Soldiering.* 1913

'Aniseed': *The Lost Herd.*

Anon: *Hunting People.* 1937

Apsley, Lady: *Bridleways through History.* 1936; *The Foxhunter's Bedside Book.* 1949

Ball, Richard: *Hounds Will Meet.* 1931

Bannisdale, V. E.: *Back to the Hills.* 1940; *Riders of the Hills.* 1939

Benson, P. G. R.: *Jingling Bits.*

Bland, E.: *Flat Racing since 1900.* 1950

Bowen, Muriel: *Irish Hunting.* 1955

Brooke, Geoffrey: *The Foxhunter's England.* 1937

Bryson, C. M. *Hunting People.* 1937

Budgett, H. M.: *Hunting by Scent.* 1933

Chalmers, Patrick R.: *The Horn. A Lay of the Grassington Foxhounds.* 1937

Charlton, Moyra: *The Echoing Horn.* 1939; *Pendellion.* 1948; *Tally Ho: The Story of an Irish Hunter.* 1930

Clapham, Richard: *The Book of the Fox.* 1936; *Foxes, Foxhounds and Fox-hunting.* 1924

'Crascredo': *Country Sense and Common Sense.* 1928; *Horse Sense and Sensibility.* 1926

Curling, B. W. R.: *British Racecourses.* 1951

Dawson, Lionel: *Sport in War.* 1936

Dewar, George A. B.: *The Pageant of English Landscape.* 1924

Fawcett, William: *Thoroughbred and Hunter.* 1934

Flint, Mark: *Grig the Greyhound.* 1938

Galtrey, S.: *The Horse in War.* 1918

'Golden Gorse': *Moorland Mousie.* 1929; *Older Mousie.* 1932

Goldschmidt, Sidney G.: *Bridle Wise.* 1927

Gordon, Adam Lindsay: *Sporting Verse.* 1927

Greaves, Ralph: *Dainty – A Foxhound.* 1948

'Heather' (Joyce M. Vivian): *Riding with Reka.* 1937

Helme, Eleanor: *Dear Busybody.* 1950; *Mayfly the Grey Pony.* 1935; *Shanks's Pony.* 1946; *Suitable Owners.* 1948; *White Winter.* 1949

Higginson, A. Henry: *As Hounds Ran. Four Centuries of Foxhunting.* 1930; *Letters from an Old Sportsman to a Younger One.* 1929; *Peter Beckford Esquire, Sportsman, Traveller and Man of Letters.* 1937

Holden, Beatrice M. B.: *They're Away.* (Poems). 1945

Kalashnikov, N.: *Jumper.* 1948

Kipling, Rudyard: *The Fox Meditates.* 1933; *The Maltese Cat.* 1936

Lyle, Robert C.: *The Aga Khan's Horses.* 1938; *Brown Jack.* 1934; *Royal Newmarket.* 1945

MacDermott, Edward T: *The Devon and Somerset Staghounds, 1907–1936.* 1936

MacKillop, J. Hutchinson, Horace G. and Dawson, Kenneth: *Letters to Young Sportsmen on Hunting, Angling and Shooting.* 1920

MacTaggart, Maxwell F.: *Mount and Man.* 1925

Mais, S. B. P.: *Hunting the Fox.* 1938

Marshall, H. J.: *Exmoor, Sporting and otherwise.* 1948

Meads, Frank: *They Meet at Eleven.* 1956

Melville, G. J. Whyte: *Songs and Verses.* 1924

Morris, Pamela Macgregor: *Exmoor Ben.* 1950; *High Honours.* 1948; *Lucky Purchase.* 1949; *Topper.* 1947

Morrison, E.: *Fox and Hare in Leicestershire.* 1954

Ogilvie, Will H.: *Collected Sporting Verse.* 1932; *Galloping Shoes.* 1922; *A Handful of Leather.* 1928; *Over the Grass.* 1925; *Scattered Scarlet.* 1923.

Pitt, Frances: *Betty.* 1943

'Rancher': *Forrard On!* 1930; *Tally Ho Back!* 1931

Roberts, Edric G.: *Somewhere in England and Other Hunting Verses.* 1929

Roderick, G.: *Gimcrack. Recollections of a Gentleman-Trainer and Rider.* 1944

Rowland, E. E.: *Hunting Songs.* 1925

'Sabretache' (A. S. Barrow): *Shires and Provinces.* 1926; *More Shires and Provinces.* 1928

Sassoon. Siegfried, and others: *My First Horse.* 1947

Sewell, Anna: *Black Beauty.* 1946

Sprigge, Elizabeth: *Pony Tracks.* 1936

Street, Arthur G.: *Country Calendar.* 1935; *Moonraking.* 1936

Trollope, Anthony: *Hunting Sketches.* 1952

Verney, Richard G., 19th Baron Willoughby de Broke: *Hunting the Fox.* 1925

Wallace, Harold F.: *A Stuart Sketch Book, 1542–1746.* Illus. by the author and by L. Edwards. 1934; *Hunting and Stalking the Deer.* 1927

Warburton, Rowland E. E.: *Hunting Songs.* 1925

Winstone, Daphne: *Flame.* 1945

INDEX